THE
Meaning
OF
Nice

To Molly: Duane,
and Matthew,
with love,
Joanie

THE
Meaning
OF
Nice

*How Compassion and
Civility Can Change Your Life
(and the World)*

JOAN DUNCAN OLIVER

BERKLEY BOOKS, NEW YORK

THE BERKLEY PUBLISHING GROUP
Published by the Penguin Group
Penguin Group (USA) Inc.
375 Hudson Street, New York, New York 10014, USA
Penguin Group (Canada), 90 Eglinton Avenue East, Suite 700, Toronto,
Ontario M4P 2Y3, Canada (a division of Pearson Penguin Canada Inc.)
Penguin Books Ltd., 80 Strand, London WC2R 0RL, England
Penguin Group Ireland, 25 St. Stephen's Green, Dublin 2, Ireland (a division of Penguin
Books Ltd.)
Penguin Group (Australia), 250 Camberwell Road, Camberwell, Victoria 3124, Australia
(a division of Pearson Australia Group Pty. Ltd.)
Penguin Books India Pvt. Ltd., 11 Community Centre, Panchsheel Park,
New Delhi—110 017, India
Penguin Group (NZ), 67 Apollo Drive, Rosedale, Auckland 0632, New Zealand
(a division of Pearson New Zealand Ltd.)
Penguin Books (South Africa) (Pty.) Ltd., 24 Sturdee Avenue, Rosebank, Johannesburg
2196, South Africa

Penguin Books Ltd., Registered Offices: 80 Strand, London WC2R 0RL, England

The publisher does not have any control over and does not assume any responsibility for
author or third-party websites or their content.

Copyright © 2012 by Joan Duncan Oliver
A complete list of credits and permissions appears on page 245.
Cover design by Sarah Oberrender
Cover photo by Getty Images / D. Sharon Pruitt, Pink Sherbet Photography
Book design by Tiffany Estreicher

PRINTING HISTORY
Berkley trade paperback edition / January 2012

Library of Congress Cataloging-in-Publication Data

Oliver, Joan Duncan.
   The meaning of nice : how compassion and civility can change your life (and the
world) / Joan Duncan Oliver.
      p. cm.
   ISBN 978-0-425-24087-8
   1. Compassion. 2. Courtesy. I. Title.
   BJ1475.O454 2012
   177'.7—dc23   2011037254

PRINTED IN THE UNITED STATES OF AMERICA

10 9 8 7 6 5 4 3 2 1

For nice people everywhere—
and all who aspire to be nicer

CONTENTS

.... ● ....

Introduction   ix

1. A Checkered Past   1

2. Nice Deconstructed   22

3. Heaven Is Other People   63

4. Why Manners Matter   98

5. Love, Love Me Do   120

6. When Kindness Goes to Work   150

7. Digital Life   164

8. Too Nice for Your Own Good   187

9. Conclusion: Are We Nice Yet?   201

Survey: The Nice Report   213

Notes   217

Acknowledgments   241

Credits   245

INTRODUCTION

So you're writing a book," a neighbor said. "What's it about?"

"Nice," I told her.

She looked puzzled. "You mean *Neece*, the city in France?"

"No, not Neece. Nice, as in ice. You know: pleasant, courteous, considerate, kind—that sort of thing. I'm exploring what makes people nice."

"But aren't you the wrong person to write about that?" she ventured.

"Are you saying I'm not nice?" I bristled.

"No, no," she said hastily. "It's just that you're from New York."

There it is: that old cliché about New Yorkers. We're rude, impatient, way too busy—and cynical—to bother being nice.

As for so-called "nice" people, they're too sweet, too accommodating to survive—much less thrive—in New York. And it's not just New Yorkers who have a stereotypic view. "I don't know how it is here in America," a friend visiting from London mused, "but in England, describing someone as nice suggests they're, well . . . rather bland."

As much as we say we value being nice, secretly we think my English friend may be right. We desperately want others to be nice to us, but we have reservations about anyone who seems too nice. We end up marrying the nice guy (or gal), but it's the naughty one whose kisses we remember long past high school.

"Isn't calling people *nice* damning them with faint praise?" another friend suggested. "A tacit admission that you can't come up with anything more interesting to say about them?" To this way of thinking, nice is safe, inoffensive, middle-of-the-road. It reminds me of a TV interview I once saw, following a screening of director Peter Bogdanovich's film *What's Up, Doc?* The movie was a screwball comedy with Barbra Streisand and Ryan O'Neal—megastars at the time—but when the screening ended, instead of applauding, the audience hissed. Bogdanovich was stunned. "What's to hiss?" he said. "That's like hissing ice cream."

In the collective unconscious, *nice* is vanilla ice cream.

Or is it? Dismissing *nice* as bland and unexciting may be as wrongheaded as assuming that all New Yorkers are rude.

Is it fair to reject out of hand a quality that is, on the face of it, so unassailable? Why do we squirm when talk turns to positive attributes? With all that's wrong in the world, shouldn't we be celebrating humanity's more admirable traits? Clearly, I thought, it's time to look deeper and give *nice* a chance.

And so I set out to examine *nice* through the lenses of philosophy, psychology, neuroscience, and religion, with input from etiquette mavens, pop culture, and common sense. As the piles of research rose on my office floor, *nice* acquired more—and sometimes surprising—meanings. By the time I had ploughed through a thicket of books, scientific studies, newspaper clips, magazine articles, and web posts, it was abundantly clear that *nice* isn't the simple Hallmark sentiment we've been led to believe but a rich broth of traits and states, values and strengths. Taken together they point, in essence, to a way of being in the world—a good-hearted approach to life, if you will.

To be sure, I was skeptical at first. In a 2010 poll, 69 percent of the respondents found Americans ruder than ever. That's down from 75 percent the previous year, but not by much. And we don't need to look far to see how ill-mannered and self-involved we've become. Trash-talking shock jocks and partisan pundits dominate the airwaves. Politicians spew vitriol; hands across the aisle are forgotten. Store clerks are surly, and customer service is nonexistent. Help lines are manned by recorded messages. The workplace is a war zone, and stressed-out workers tote their frustrations home. Children bully their classmates and order their parents around. There's an epidemic of hate crimes, and entitlement is the new social disease.

Considering how pervasive bad behavior is today, it was a challenge to focus on what's nice. It's easier to look at what isn't *nice* than what is. And what do we mean by *nice* anyway? In a brief survey I circulated among family, friends, and friends of friends, I listed sixty adjectives and asked participants to tick off the ones they most associated with *nice*. What emerged as the overall winner was *kind*. No surprise there, but what did surprise me were some related findings: although *kind* was the first choice among the men, the number one pick for the women was *courteous*—a word that didn't even make it into the men's top ten. Manners do matter to at least half the world, it seems—even if we don't always act like we mean it.

A physical therapist who moved to the United States from Canada told me, "I think Canadians are more polite than Americans. But," he quickly added, "that doesn't mean they're nicer." Courtesy alone can't qualify us as nice. If it could, we would have no trouble building a nation of nice people: just make etiquette classes mandatory in elementary school, beginning with first grade.

So if nice isn't about holding doors and giving the elderly

your seat on the bus, what exactly does it consist of? We'll explore the possibilities in detail in the following pages, but it's clear that nice has a number of meanings, depending on who's looking at it and from what angle. On balance, niceness seems to be an ingrained response. Ingrained, but not innate. While there is mounting evidence that traits like compassion and empathy are inborn, being nice is a largely acquired skill that anyone can learn. What's inborn is the *capacity* for niceness. After that, family, friends, school, community, and religion—aided by intelligence, persistence, and self-awareness—work in tandem to hone the talent.

One sign of our growing interest in humanity's more salubrious side is the rise of positive psychology, which emphasizes the good in human nature rather than the pathological, psychology's focus since the field began. Positive psychologists have identified twenty-four measurable character strengths that are found, in varying combinations and to varying degrees, in mature, mentally stable people. As we'll see in chapter 2, Nice Deconstructed, these strengths and virtues are not only the building blocks of happiness but also markers for identifying the people and behavior most likely to be labeled *nice*.

The roots of *nice* run deeper than personality. Character is the key. Not that genuinely nice people are goody-goodies. Like anyone, they stumble on occasion, but there's a strain of decency underneath. Perhaps the best way of characterizing a nice person is the word *mensch*. German for "human being," *mensch* in Yiddish means so much more. "The key to being a 'real mensch'," Leo Rosten explains in *The New Joys of Yiddish*, "is nothing less than character: rectitude, dignity, a sense of what is right, responsible, decorous." The Encarta dictionary defines a mensch as "somebody good, kind, decent, and honorable." A mensch is someone "you would be happy to befriend and associate with because you feel genuine in [his] presence," adds JewishLink, an online resource on Jewish healing and spirituality, in "The Art of the Mensch." But it's with this definition that JewishLink really brings the idea home: "A person is a mensch because he simply makes others feel good." What could be nicer than that?

Qualities like integrity, honesty, loyalty, and compassion take *nice* beyond the one-dimensional, what's-to-hiss meaning previously assigned to it. But before we look closely at *nice*'s salutary meanings, we need to acknowledge its darker side. "Oh, nice," we snap sarcastically when someone does something really stupid or messes up big time. And in the obverse world of urban slang, nice means just the opposite: "Yo, man, she nice" translates as "She's a real badass." So nice hasn't always meant sweetness and light. In fact, the word has a checkered past, as we'll discover in chapter 1. It has taken nearly a millennium for *nice* to get to where it is now.

But for all that, is there anything about *nice* that has existed down through time and across all cultures? Indeed, there are certain qualities we associate with nice people, such as caring and compassion, that seem to be shared by people the world over, whether they are African nomads, South Seas Islanders, or West Texas teens.

Being nice, in the first instance, is a solo activity—no one can be nice for you. Yet for anyone except perhaps a monk on solitary retreat, *nice* is a social matter. Whether I'm nice or nasty affects the world around me—even when I think that no one is watching. We are always in some sort of interaction with the human or built or natural environment. Chapter 3, Heaven Is Other People, explores *nice* as an interpersonal endeavor.

Perhaps nowhere is nice behavior more of an issue than in our intimate relations. We grant family special privileges, but often in a negative way: somehow we find it OK to be rude, angry, or selfish with our own flesh and blood. As Robert Frost famously put it, "Home is the place where, when you have to go there, they have to take you in." But do the truly nice have one set of behaviors for the world at large and another, lesser set for the people they love? How do nice people deal with the inevitable arguments and misunderstandings of intimate life? Future chapters look at these questions in the context of love relationships, friendship, and manners.

Work is another area where nice—and not-so-nice—behavior stands out. It's a dog-eat-dog world, the prevailing work ethic tells us, so you had better bite or be bitten. But as chapter 6, When Kindness Goes to Work, suggests, there is heartening news from the workplace. Certain individuals are bringing enlightened values to the office, and whole companies and industries are moving toward more humane ways of doing business.

Doing well by doing good is gaining favor as a private ethos, as well. Volunteering—niceness in action—is on the upswing. There is increased awareness that who we are and how we live impacts not just our own backyards and communities but people and ecosystems around the world. Sometimes it takes a celebrity—a Bill Gates or a Bill Clinton or a George Clooney—to focus our attention on suffering at a distance, but thanks to twenty-first century global communications, we're exposed to exemplars of kindness and generosity wherever they're found. We learn to be nice by watching others.

Which brings us back to manners. Etiquette may not be the whole story when it comes to being nice, but manners are not peripheral to our lives, as chapter 4, Why Manners Matter, reveals. Manners broadcast who we are at any given time, a fact not lost on a group of inner-city teens who wrote a hip-hop etiquette guide for their peers. "Manners say, 'You can count on me,'" observes Mary Landers, the teacher who supervised the project.

But count on me for what, exactly? If this were medieval Europe, I might say "for not stabbing you at dinner"—a very real concern in those days. In today's world, trustworthy behavior might include such things as not stealing your client, or your spouse, or the taxi you're hailing. Manners announce our intention not to knowingly hurt others, and express our commitment to be honest, courteous, and sensitive to one another's needs. At the very least, manners are like clean clothes: they make a good impression and show respect. Nearly all the Nice Survey respondents counted manners important or very important. But in rating their own performance in the manners department, all but a handful called it average at best. Is that modesty—or a frank acknowledgment of the discrepancy in today's world between values and behavior?

These days, it's not unusual to find people who are kindness personified and generous to a fault, yet who routinely answer their cell phones or check for text messages in the middle of meetings and social gatherings, even at the dinner table. With their phones and iPads turned off, these people seem adrift, as if something critical is missing. It is. We're in thrall to our digital companions—and it's only going to get worse. With every new gadget and upgrade, there is less and less incentive to separate ourselves from our electronic partners for even a nanosecond. But is anyone asking, *Is this nice?* Chapter 7, Digital Life, looks at electronic communications and social networking, and our growing tendency to put these relationships before face-to-face encounters.

*   *   *

All this brings us back to the central question of *The Meaning of Nice*: What does it mean to be nice in today's world—and how important is it anyway? A number of Nice Survey participants said that filling out the questionnaire was the first time they had given serious thought to being nice and to whether or not they—and the people around them—were making the grade. (To find out where you stand, see the Nice Survey on page 213, or online at www.thenicereport.net.)

Despite all the attention our bad behavior has received, there is evidence that nicer, kinder behavior is poised for a comeback. Not long ago, an upscale tabloid, the *New York Observer*, dropped its usual snarky tone to herald the shift in an issue headlined "The New Nice." That same month, *Harper's Bazaar* ran an essay by the actress Rita Wilson proclaiming, "Nice Is the New Black." And a few months before that, *Vogue* published "The Kindness Project," an article that grew out of writer Miranda Purves's decision to, as she put it, "make it through the holidays with my family without a single mean outburst." It's an aspiration shared by many. For advice, Purves had phoned London psychoanalyst Adam Phillips, co-author of *On Kindness*, a surprise best seller in 2009.

So why is *nice* on the collective radar? Is being nice indeed "the new black": hip, au courant, yet classic—right for all occasions? Are we seeing a course correction in behavior, or just a momentary backlash against the me-first-ism that has overrun the culture in recent years?

We could just as well ask the question another way: What made nice behavior fall out of favor in the first place? Presuming, of course, that nice has had its historical moments. Whatever the rising and falling fortunes of the word *nice* down through the years, notions of virtue and character have been around since the Hellenic era. (Chapter 1, A Checkered Past, explores the relationship between the nice and the good.) The people who embody super-nice behavior today—such as His Holiness the Dalai Lama, widely considered the nicest person on the planet—are in many ways just big-screen examples of the native human capacity for compassion, courtesy, kindness, generosity, and forgiveness. Every village, every community has its local heroes—people who are noticeably caring and supportive.

So when did the nice train go off the rails? How come *consistently* nice behavior has been so hard to find in recent years? Did the post–World War II melting pot stir in so many new voices and expectations that traditional manners and mores fell out of favor? Does responsibility rest with the sixties counterculture, who rejected anything identified with authority or the Establishment? Did the Me Generation of the 1970s trade being nice for finding oneself? Or is the problem the balkanization of family life ushered in by the two-career household? Was the *coup de grace* to *nice* delivered by the rise of the Internet and the too-much-information era?

Don't blame the Internet, a friend told me over coffee at Starbucks, scanning his text messages between sentences and bites of his croissant. In fact, he claimed, it's the Internet that's responsible for the nice revival, bringing us together in the vast village square of cyberspace while collapsing old barriers of age, race, religion, class, gender, and whatever. "But hasn't digital togetherness gone a bit too far?" I countered. "Hasn't Facebook steamrollered over quaint notions like courtesy and privacy, not to mention the intimacy of actually sitting down with one another?"

My friend snickered, but still I wondered. What about the new-media holdouts, or the small but growing minority questioning the idea that living out loud and online 24/7 is necessary or desirable? Now that every utterance, every unflattering photo, every dumb thing we've ever done hangs forever in the cloud, wouldn't we want to be more circumspect about what we say and do? Aren't some things better left unseen and unsaid? The privacy train may have already left the station, but it's not too late to develop a modicum of discretion.

Even as we redefine *nice* for the new millennium, there are pockets of restraint. Online, it's as simple as people "defriend-ing" people they don't actually know, and cutting back on tweets or dropping Twitter altogether. (Does anybody's life really warrant minute-to-minute revelations to a million followers?) Offline, meanwhile, there's an uptick in old-fashioned social involvement: friends getting together in real time and place, book discussion groups and crafting circles springing up, families having meals together. Character and values are once again conversational topics—and not just among radical right-wingers attempting to turn back time. Even grade-schoolers are learning the importance of living together peacefully and responsibly on the planet.

The fact is, beneath all our pettiness and self-concern, we humans are caring creatures. That's the message of ancient spiritual teachings and of modern science, as neuroscientists probe brain centers that light up when we're compassionate or generous. Current research confirms that kind people have an easier time in the world, not least in terms of health, emotional well-being, and relations with others. And when a group of centenarians was interviewed by *The New York Times* on the key to their longevity, they predictably cited factors like genes, healthy habits, and having fun. But one woman chalked it up to a positive outlook: "I always put anything disagreeable or bad out of the way. That's the secret of life. Don't emphasize anything that is evil or bad, but get rid of it or rise above it."

Being nice may not guarantee long life—there are those pesky genes and fitness habits to consider. But it can make the journey richer and more rewarding, whatever its length.

···················· ◆ ····················

Chapter One

A Checkered Past

Wouldn't you know, it was the French who gave us the word *nice*. But they weren't very nice about it, at least in the way we think of *nice* today—"delightful, agreeable, a general epithet of approval or commendation," as *The Oxford English Dictionary* puts it. *Nice* comes from *neyce,* Old French for foolish or stupid, which itself derives from the Latin *nescire*, to be ignorant or undiscerning. Call someone *neyce* in the thirteenth century and you were calling him a fool.

So how did we get from *neyce* to *nice*, from foolish to agreeable and delightful? By all accounts, it wasn't easy. The authors of *The Private Lives of English Words* tell us that since it was introduced into Middle English from Old French back in the 1300s, *nice* has undergone more twists and turns in meaning that almost any other word in the English language.

In fact, the etymological wanderings of *nice* take up five densely packed columns in the OED, which cautions against looking for any logical progression. Duly warned, we can forge ahead.

As *neyce* was ferried across the English Channel from France, it morphed into *nyce*, and the English latched onto its meaning as silly or stupid with a flourish. *The Romance of William of Palerne*, a French work translated into English, offers a choice example: "Now witterly ich am vn-wise & wonderliche nyce"—"I am unwise and wondrously foolish." Chaucer heartily embraced *nice* in *The Canterbury Tales*, giving the word a second meaning—"wanton, loose-mannered, lascivious"—that only added to its disrepute. *The Romance of the Rose*, a French work that Chaucer reputedly helped translate into English, describes a nice woman of the day: "Nyce she was, but she mente ne Noon harme ne slight in hir entente, but oonely lust & jolyte"—"Loose-mannered she was, but she meant no one harm nor [was] slight her intent, only lust and jollity."

By the 1400s, *nice-as-wanton* had spawned yet another meaning: "coy, shy, affectedly modest." *The Romance of Sir Beues of Hamtoun* introduces a bride of that era: "maydens at her first weddying, Wel nyse al þhe first nyht."—"maiden at her first wedding; well shy on the first night." And *nice* didn't stop there. It also described someone "extravagant" or "flaunting," particularly in dress.

By the 1500s, *nice* was gathering new meanings with abandon, acquiring a veneer of respectability when "dainty," "fastidious," "refined," and "too delicate" were added to the list. Thomas More, in *Utopia,* describes a nice man of the time as "of so nyce and soo delycate a mynde that he settethe nothynge by it"—"of so nice and delicate a mind that he sets nothing by it." Not that *nice* had shed its risqué associations altogether. *Nice Wanton*, a popular morality play that served as sex education for Renaissance teens, graphically lays out the dangers of promiscuity through the warning example of a young woman who dies of the pox—that is, syphilis.

By the seventeenth century *nice* was in full flower. Shakespeare commandeered it for a variety of uses. In *Henry V,* for one, *nice* means "overly refined": King Henry, wooing Catherine, daughter of France's monarch, suggests that she—and he—are far superior to the fussy conventions of the French court: "O Kate, nice customs curtsy to great kings ... [but] you and I cannot be confined within the weak list of a country's fashion." *Nice* continued to be attached to women of dubious reputation—the "nice wenches" in *Love's Labour's Lost*, for example—but at the same time it was also starting to mean just the opposite: "scrupulous" and "unsullied." The satirist Jonathan Swift, waxing serious in his tract *A Project for the Advancement of Religion and the Reformation of Manners,* rails against what he sees as a laxity in the morals of the time: "How comes it to pass that women of tainted reputations find the same countenance and reception in all public places with those of the nicest virtue, who pay and receive visits from them without any manner of scruple?"

But it wasn't until the latter part of the eighteenth century and the dawn of the Romantic era that *nice* underwent a thorough laundering, largely shedding its shady past to attach itself to gentler—and more genteel—people and behavior. Now *nice* was identified with qualities like "tasteful," "agreeable," and "pleasing to others." In the Gothic potboiler *The Mysteries of Udolpho*—a huge bestseller following its 1794 publication—Ann Radcliffe captures the rosy glow surrounding *nice* in describing her young heroine: "Lovely as was her person, it was the varied experience of her countenance, as conversation awakened the nicer emotions of her mind, that threw such a captivating grace around her."

Now we're entering more familiar territory. Chaucer's lusty wench has mellowed into a sweet young thing. And *nice* wasn't reserved just for ladies of that era: men, too, could revel in its glow. But beware a snake in the grass: for all its newly acquired agreeableness, *nice* soon had its detractors—as it does to this day. From this point on, the use of *nice* as "agreeable" and "delightful" is "frequently somewhat derisive," the OED tells us.

Jane Austen, ever the deft chronicler of social manners, quietly skewers *nice* in *Northanger Abbey*. Teasing the impressionable Catherine Morland for calling *The Mysteries of Udol-*

pho "the nicest book in the world," the young clergyman Henry Tilney riffs on *nice*: "Oh, it is a very nice word, indeed!— it does for everything. Originally, perhaps it was applied only to express neatness, propriety, delicacy, or refinement— people were nice in their dress, in their sentiments, or their choice. But now every commendation on every subject is comprised in that one word."

And the undoing of *nice* didn't stop there. In the two centuries since *Northanger Abbey* was published, other authors have pilloried the word, not least for the cloying aftertaste that too much niceness leaves. No question, *nice* invites irony. Charles Dickens wrote to his about-to-be-former boss, the owner of a magazine Dickens had been editing, to say, "I have been clearing off all the rejected articles to-day, and nice work I have had." Plowing through the manuscripts in the reject pile, any editor will tell you, can be about as "nice" as Dante's visit to hell.

Still, it took the dawn of the twentieth century to finally drive a stake through nice. In *The House of Mirth*, Edith Wharton writes of Lawrence Selden, who's in love with the decidedly unconventional Lily Bart: "There had been a germ of truth in his declaration . . . that he had never wanted to marry a 'nice' girl; the adjective connoting . . . certain utilitarian qualities which are apt to preclude the luxury of charm."

So much for the foolish or wanton woman, or the captivating young thing: nice girls circa 1905 were just plain dull. In

1926, the great usage maven H. W. Fowler essentially deleted *nice* from the list of acceptable adjectives in one stroke when he declared that the word "has been too great a favorite of the ladies, who have charmed out of it all its individuality and converted it into a mere diffuser of vague and mild agreeableness."

Ouch. Could nice ever recover from such a charge of insipidness? Amazingly, it not only could but did. Admittedly, *nice* continues to drag along baggage: the ragtag assortment of definitions the word has accumulated through the centuries hasn't disappeared altogether. And hackneyed expressions like "Have a nice day" and "He's such a nice guy" haven't helped *nice*'s image either. But as we intimated in the introduction, there's every reason to think *nice* is regaining favor—in its best iteration, at least. Not the foolish or wanton *nice* of Chaucer's day or the saccharine, convention-bound *nice* that Austen, Dickens, Wharton, and Fowler eviscerated. The new *nice* is an estimable quality, a cloak of kindness to wrap around ourselves in a cold, cruel world. Something good to be—and good to be around.

But what does it mean to be nice in the twenty-first century? On what basis can we argue that a much-disparaged and seemingly innocuous quality is, in reality, rich in positive meaning? Clearly, just tracing the meanderings of the word doesn't tell the whole story of what is nice today in people and behavior. Where else should we look?

To philosophy and religion for a start.

Long before we worried about being nice, we worried about being good. For thousands of years, philosophers and spiritual leaders have been asking questions like "What does it mean to be a human being?" and "How should we live?" Every religion and philosophy—every group, in fact—has some code of conduct built in, some definition of what it considers right. If we're looking for qualities that characterize nice people, virtue—moral excellence—would be a place to start. More than winning ways or a charming smile, virtue is what makes us admirable and upstanding: nice for the long haul, not just for the moment.

But what about that word *virtue*? I can already hear the groans. For one thing, the word has been co-opted by right-wing extremists to imply righteous, God-fearing, and whatever else they think the rest of us are not. Then, too, for some people virtue talk taps into memories of stern nuns or hellfire preachers threatening eternal damnation for dancing too close at the prom. Even without that sort of baggage, virtue can seem oppressive, an impossible ideal—some standard of behavior that us ordinary mortals couldn't possibly aspire to. Or wouldn't want to. "I far prefer silent vice to ostentatious virtue," Albert Einstein allegedly said. Whether or not he actually said it, the sentiment is widespread. Virtue has a bad reputation, but in truth, it isn't reserved for the devout or angelic. It couldn't be more grounded in the here and now. The origin of the word is *virtus,* Latin for manliness, strength, and worth. At one time, virtue meant valor. Virtue, then, is robust, proactive, teeming with vitality. It's the kick in the pants that makes us achieve great things and do what's right. And if we consider the virtues, what are they but qualities like kindness, honesty, and generosity that we find meritorious in people the world over?

So where did our ideas about virtue come from? And when did the good and the nice hook up? To find out, we need to go back a few thousand years, to ancient Greece. It's doubtful the early Greeks sat around the *agora,* the marketplace, debating what it means to be nice. For one thing, there was no such word as *nice* in the vocabulary of fifth- and sixth-century BCE Athens. But that doesn't mean that the philosophers of the day weren't concerned with character. Virtue is the key to well-being, they held. For the early Greeks moral excellence was both the seed and the fruit of the good life—unquestionably something to strive for.

To Aristotle, *eudaimonia*—well-being or flourishing—was "the end and aim of human life," the highest human good. The way to achieve it is through character development, he said. We're not born virtuous, he argued, but we have the capacity for it; we become virtuous by doing virtuous things. Just as practicing the harp produces a harpist, "moral excellence is the product of habit," Aristotle declared. The key to the good life is moderation in all things—sticking to the moral mean between "excess and deficiency." Generosity, for example, is the mean between stinginess and prodigality; courage the mean between overconfidence and fear. Every virtue also has its attendant vices, according to Aristotle, and it's up to each individual to arrive at a personal calculus for achieving a balance. Having discovered "the errors to which we are personally prone," we should then bend ourselves "in the opposite direction, for by steering wide of error we shall strike a middle course, as warped timber is straightened by bending it backwards." Reason will guide us to the good. Not that Aristotle was against emotion. He was all for it—as long as it was expressed "at the right times, with reference to the right objects, toward the right people, with the right motive, and in the right manner." Daunting as that sounds, it still stands as sage advice for maintaining inner peace and harmonious relations with others.

Maintaining good relations with others was important to the Greeks. They considered friendship an acid test of moral fiber. To Aristotle, the ideal friend doesn't nurse grudges or speak ill of others and is good-tempered, tactful, and "morally good." The purpose of friendship, he said, is to give, not get. A real friend wants above all for his friends to flourish: "We may describe friendly feeling toward anyone as wishing for him what you believe to be good things, not for your own sake, but his."

The ancient Romans also touted the importance of virtue. Moral goodness is the cement that holds society together, the poet/statesman Cicero held. To Cicero, the key virtues were justice, which keeps us from harming one another, and charity—kindness and generosity—which guides us in giving and receiving, and respecting others. The worst form of injustice, Cicero held, is hypocrisy—pretending to be virtuous when we're not—while our greatest duty is to be grateful for generosity we receive. Like Aristotle, Cicero prized friendship: those displaying "moral goodness" would naturally gravitate toward one another, he said.

Another Roman whose thoughts on character still inspire us is Marcus Aurelius, the last of the great Roman emperors. "Waste no more time arguing about what a good man should be," he said. "Be one."

While the Greeks and Romans were ruminating on what makes us virtuous, in the East teachers like Confucius and the Buddha had already laid out guidelines for right living. The Buddha wasn't a moralizer, nor was he concerned with philosophizing: his goal was to help us struggling human beings rise above our perpetual dissatisfaction—our eternal frustration at not getting what we want, or getting what we don't want, or losing what we have. Like Aristotle, the Buddha taught that the path to self-awareness and happiness lies in the middle way between self-indulgence and self-denial. Character development is the key, he said. Through cultivating such qualities as generosity, patience, loving-kindness, and equanimity, we awaken to our true nature as wise and compassionate beings. Buddhism's exemplar of the good person is the *bodhisattva,* one who takes a selfless vow to help all beings attain inner freedom.

Confucius, too, laid out a path of virtuous living emphasizing, as he put it, "moral force." His exemplar, the superior man, "in everything considers righteousness to be essential." Confucius identified more than fifty virtues we should cultivate, from kindness, generosity, and broad-mindedness to loyalty and respect for family. But the supreme virtue and sum of them all, he said, is *jen*—"humaneness"—the essence of which is to love all humanity. "Virtue is not left to stand alone," he said. "He who practices it will have neighbors." To Confucius, a good person is one who is gentle, sincere, and diligent; who, when angry, reflects on the consequences; and who, when given an opportunity for self-gain, proceeds with caution. Asked to single out one overriding principle to live by, Confucius was unequivocal: "What you do not wish for yourself, do not impose on others."

There it is, the Golden Rule. Some variation on it exists in nearly all the world's moral teachings. Whether it is grounded in the notion of reciprocity ("You scratch my back, I'll scratch yours") or a sense of fair play ("Everyone should be treated equally") or compassion ("Love thy neighbor as you love yourself"), the Golden Rule is, for many, the bottom line for living a virtuous life.

"One should never do that to another which one regards as injurious to one's own self," says the *Mahabharata*, one of Hinduism's sacred texts. "This, in brief, is the rule of dharma." It sounds remarkably like something the great Jewish Rabbi Hillel said. When a pagan told Hillel he would convert to Judaism if Hillel could stand on one leg and recite the whole of Jewish teaching, Hillel stood on one leg and told him, "That which is hateful to you, do not do to your neighbor. That is the whole Torah; the rest is commentary."

Both the Old and New Testaments offer myriad teachings on cultivating virtue. For the early Jews, virtue came from walking in the way of God and obeying the Ten Commandments. To this day observant Jews follow the prophet Isaiah's prescription for the good life: "Cease to do evil, learn to do good; seek justice, correct oppression; defend the fatherless, plead for the widow."

For Christians, Jesus is the essence of goodness and the quintessential Mr. Nice Guy: forthright, charismatic, inspiring, generous, compassionate, and fair. Being good the Christian way means avoiding the seven deadly sins—pride, envy, gluttony, lust, anger, greed, and sloth—and practicing the seven virtues: faith, hope, charity, fortitude, justice, prudence, and temperance. Anyone who has attended parochial school probably has also learned the seven contrary virtues as a hedge against the seven deadly sins: humility to overcome pride; kindness to counter envy; abstinence to quash gluttony; chastity to quell lust; patience to quiet anger; generosity to conquer greed; and diligence to shake off sloth.

By the Middle Ages, the chivalric code was in full force as the standard of conduct, and the knight in shining armor was the model of good character. Virtues like loyalty, courtesy, generosity, and concern for those in need were essential bows in the knight's moral quiver. Along with fidelity to God, they defined the ideal for medieval Europe. Books like *Le Livre de Chevalier de la Tour Landry*, written by a French knight in the late fourteenth century, offer the sort of moral education that parents of the day passed along to their children. In this case, the advice was aimed at the knight's daughters, schooling them in the virtues of courtesy, modesty, chastity, and marital fidelity, while warning them—in lurid detail—of the dire fate awaiting those who give in to sexual temptation.

Medieval Christian clerics, for their part, had plenty to say about proper conduct. But as the Middle Ages wound down and the Renaissance gathered steam, religion lost its iron grip on behavior. Being good was no longer a matter of deferring to God's will but to the king's.

The Italian and French aristocracy devised elaborate rules for good behavior that filtered down to the newly emerging bourgeoisie and eventually to the masses. "Courtesy books"—from *curteis,* Old French for "courtly"—were enormously popular, detailing proper conduct through exemplars of noble birth. Just as Aristotle and Confucius had laid ethical foundations for right living, the courtesy books promoted virtues of a slightly different sort. The English pored over translations of sixteenth-century writers like Giovanni Della Casa and Baldassare Castiglione, whose works set standards of behavior for centuries to come. Della Casa's *Il Galateo* is filled with pronouncements like: "It is a rude fashion . . . that some men use, to lye lolling asleepe in that place where honest men be met together of purpose to talke. . . . But they are much more to bee blamed, that pull out theyr knyves or their scisers, and doe nothing else but pare their nayles."

If that sounds more like Miss Manners than *Lives of the Saints*, it suggests that the realm of the good was beginning to drift in a more worldly direction. Manners as we know them hadn't yet earned a seat at the table alongside the virtues, but they were not incidental. As Della Casa put it, being "polite, pleasant, and well-mannered" in dealing with others, if not a virtue, is "something similar"—and daily life provides at least as many opportunities to trot out good manners as to exercise virtues like courage and generosity.

Il Galateo and Castiglione's *Il Cortegiano* (*The Book of the Courtier*) were never intended to be mere instruction manuals for behavior, however. At bottom, they set out the conditions of good character. *Il Cortegiano*, based on the author's keen observations of life at the court of Urbino, details the qualities of the ideal courtier. It's a dizzying list that runs the gamut from athletic prowess and skill in weaponry to fluency in foreign languages and mastery of all the arts. On top of that, the courtier was to be handsome, well dressed, informed on current events, diplomatic to a fault, and then some. "To avoid envy and to keep company pleasantly with every man," wrote Castiglione, "let [the courtier] do whatsoever other men do: so he declines not at any time from commendable deeds but governs himself with that good judgment that will not suffer him to enter into any folly: but let him laugh, dally, jest, and dance, yet in such ways that he may always declare himself to be witty and discreet, and everything that he does or speaks, let him do it with a grace."

It was Louis XIV, however, who pushed courtly behavior to dizzying heights of refinement, with precepts that owed more to style than moral substance. During his sixty-two-year reign, which ran well into the eighteenth century, France's Sun King defined mores that were breathtaking in their elaboration. The word *etiquette*—meaning the rules of socially acceptable behavior—comes from the Old French word *estiquet,* or ticket, referring to little cards posted at Versailles or given out to the courtiers reminding them what to do and not do, down to "Keep off the grass."

A century later, across the Atlantic, settlers in the fledgling American republic were throwing off the shackles of European court behavior and devising their own ideas about proper conduct. Some rebelled against anything that smacked of the old ways, insisting that so-called "manners" had nothing to do with ordinary life. Others disagreed. As historian Arthur Schlesinger argues in his survey of American etiquette books, "Manners, far from being apart from life, are veritably a part of life, revealing men's hopes, standards, and strivings."

One of the country's earliest strivers was George Washington. As a youth, he copied down a list of 110 "Rules of Civility and Decent Behavior in Company and Conversation" that he then set out to live by. Said to be based on a code of conduct formulated by French Jesuits in the sixteenth century, Washington's rules not only include the usual injunctions against rude and crude behavior—don't bite your nails, don't cough without covering your mouth, don't scratch your private parts at the table, and so on—but also spell out precepts that go to the heart of being good. Washington was well known as upstanding and considerate of others, and a moral thread runs through his list. Injunctions like be modest, associate with good company, don't gossip or meddle in others' affairs, and don't gloat over others' misfortune are the sort of proscriptions that define good character in any era. Washington's precepts represent the cumulative wisdom of moral history, summed up in his Rule 1: "Every action done in Company, ought to be with Some Sign of Respect, to those that are Present." To this day, Washington's Rule 1 is, for many, the sine qua non of an upright life.

Another famous early American, Benjamin Franklin, also

committed early in life to being a better person. Among his inspirations was the *Distichs of Cato*, a collection of homilies by a third- or fourth-century CE scholar that served as a popular Latin textbook from the Middle Ages on. With advice like "If you can, even remember to help people you don't know. / More precious than a kingdom it is to gain friends by kindness," Cato provided moral guidance to centuries of impressionable youth.

In his autobiography, Franklin explains in some detail his "Bold and arduous Project of arriving at moral Perfection," based on breaking old habits and building new ones. The virtues he espoused are timeless, and with the possible exception of his prohibition against sex for anything but "Health or Offspring," so are his precepts for mastering them. To develop humility, the thirteenth and last quality on Franklin's list, "Imitate Jesus and Socrates," he suggests. Franklin's catalogue of guidelines lays out an exemplary path to the moral high ground:

1. **Temperance.** Eat not to Dullness. Drink not to Elevation.

2. **Silence.** Speak not but what may benefit others or yourself. Avoid trifling Conversation.

3. **Order.** Let all your Things have their Places. Let each Part of your Business have its Time.

4. **Resolution.** Resolve to perform what you ought. Perform without fail what you resolve.

5. **Frugality.** Make no Expense but to do good to others or yourself: i.e. Waste nothing.

6. **Industry.** Lose no time. Be always employ'd in something useful. Cut off all unnecessary Actions.

7. **Sincerity.** Use no hurtful Deceit. Think innocently and justly; and, if you speak, speak accordingly.

8. **Justice.** Wrong none, by doing Injuries or omitting the Benefits that are your Duty.

9. **Moderation.** Avoid extremes. Forbear resenting Injuries so much as you think they deserve.

10. **Cleanliness.** Tolerate no Uncleanness in Body, Clothes, or Habitation.

11. **Tranquillity.** Be not disturbed at Trifles, or at Accidents common or unavoidable.

12. **Chastity.** Rarely use Venery [sexual intercourse] but for Health or Offspring; Never to Dullness, Weakness, or the Injury of your own or another's Peace or Reputation.

13. **Humility.** Imitate Jesus and Socrates.

By the nineteenth century, self-improvement guides like Washington's and Franklin's were disappearing, and "conduct books" were all the rage. Rather than pitching the virtues directly, they offered tutorials in what Sarah J. Hale, in her 1867 manual, *Manners; or, Happy Homes and Good Society All the Year Around*, called "the power of the littles": "It is not the great things which give the effect; it is the little things— the graceful finishing touches," she wrote. "It is only the frivolous, and those who have been superficially educated, or only instructed in showy accomplishments, who despise and neglect the ordinary duties of life as beneath their notice."

Mrs. Hale's standards of conduct—and by extension, her vehicles for building character—were not confined to house and home. Even what we wear has a higher purpose beyond warmth and comfort, she ventured. "Dress is the index of conscience, the evidence of our emotional nature. It reveals, more clearly than speech expresses, the inner life of heart and soul in a people, and also the tendencies of individual character." (Try telling that to your teenager the next time she leaves the house in too much makeup and too few clothes.)

The idea of clothes-as-character wasn't such a far-fetched proposition, however. There were precedents. In the sixteenth century, a Dutch scholar, Erasmus of Rotterdam, went so far as to say that he could deduce, from specific items of clothing, the wearer's spiritual condition. Students at Louis

D. Brandeis High School in New York evoked shades of Erasmus and Mrs. Hale in *Etiquette—Our Way: A Teen Guide to Appropriate Behavior*, a book they drafted under the guidance of their English teacher, Mary Landers. "If you have rolls"—of fat, that is—"do not wear shirts that sit on the rolls or barely cover them," the teens advise. "Appropriate behavior and presentation of self is what etiquette is all about. It is an opportunity for someone's character to shine forth."

Even Ralph Waldo Emerson, éminence grise of American letters, weighed in on the moral significance of appearance. He, too, argued that how we look and behave betrays our character. "There is no beautifier of complexion, or form, or behavior, like the wish to scatter joy and not pain around us," he said. To Emerson, the good and the nice were clearly one.

It's questionable whether the people who flock to the etiquette section of the bookstore chains today are consciously out to scatter joy. But we have to assume that at least some are concerned with more than just where to seat Grandmother at the bridal dinner, even if that something more is, in the best Emersonian sense, not to scatter pain. For as we'll see, Emerson is hardly alone in sensing an inextricable connection between the good and the nice, virtue and good manners. Instead of dismissing etiquette as the frivolous cousin of character, a handful of academics are starting to view them as equal partners. "Ethics, the practice of living a good life, has always depended on the graceful relations for which etiquette provides a ticket to enter the domain of sociability," argue Rob Scapp and Brian Setz in the introduction to their anthology, *Etiquette: Reflections on Contemporary Comportment.*

So if, as Aristotle suggested, living a virtuous life makes us good, does this mean that being good makes us nice? Perhaps that's asking the wrong question. The satirist P. J. O'Rourke puts the whole business of virtue and behavior in perspective with this observation: "Good manners can replace morals. It may be years before anyone knows if what you are doing is right. But if what you are doing is nice, it will be immediately evident."

Chapter Two

.... ◆ ....

Nice Deconstructed

What do we think *nice* is today? Who are the people who exemplify it? We're no longer wench-chasing Elizabethans or swooning eighteenth-century romantics, so we're unlikely to be searching for *nice* at either extreme. The pendulum has swung far from the *nyce*-but-naughty that drew winks from Chaucer and Shakespeare—but not so far that we're worshipping decorum like eminent Victorians.

In chapter 1 we saw evidence that over the centuries the good devolved into the nice. The virtues the ancients touted as worthy and admirable were gradually replaced by wispier attributes like charisma and charm. As virtue fell out of favor—a casualty of modernity—psychology became the new guiding star. Now human beings were defined in scientific terms: we emerged as a collection of traits, motivations, emotions, and behaviors. Given that, it might be easier to identify *nice* if it were an emotion like joy or trust or fear—even easier if it were a heritable trait like blue eyes or wavy hair. But whenever we try to pinpoint niceness in anyone, the trait *qua* trait disappears into thin air. We're forced to conclude that niceness is not a single trait but a collection of traits—or broader still, a multidimensional skill for living.

Kate Middleton, the commoner who landed a king-to-be, is to many the quintessential nice girl for the twenty-first century: genteel, decorous, polite, industrious, kind, and unfailingly loyal. Her transformation into Catherine, Duchess of Cambridge, is hailed as a triumph of middle-class values—work hard, have a sunny disposition, don't make a scene, and you'll succeed. Whatever passions roil within the newly minted royal are tucked away neatly behind a cloak of propriety and a gracious smile. Careful never to put a foot wrong, she's the envy of countless young women around the globe—and not just because she's living the fairy tale. "Kate is straightforward, really nice, composed, feminine," a wedding guest who once worked with her told a reporter. "Discreet and quiet, but with a strong sense of herself. She's a really classy girl." Catherine/Kate is also a product of the very British notion of moving forward by building on the best of the past. As social critic and *New York Times* columnist David Brooks described it, the British style of change "emphasizes modesty, gradualism, and balance." Princess Diana, by contrast, went all out for a radical overthrow of the monarchy—or at least its mustier traditions—an approach that, not surprisingly, did not sit well with the royal family.

Is *nice* today, then, circumscribed by a calm disposition, respect for the past, and impeccable manners? Surely there's more to it than that. Etiquette manuals and how-to books on landing a job or a mate can take us only so far. So how will we characterize *nice* in our crass, bullying, reality-show culture? Psychological literature is largely mute on the subject, but there's a substantial body of research on "likability"— likableness, if you prefer. The word alone is rife with associations, suggesting that likability might play more than a walk-on role in defining *nice*. It's possible to think someone is nice but not to like him—we all know people who fall into this category, even family members at times—but it's improbable to think someone is nice but *unlikable*.

What, then, does likability consist of? It's a popular topic with management consultants, therapists, Internet pundits, and anyone else dispensing advice on how to get ahead. In a blog post headed "Cultivating your Inner Jennifer Aniston: 9 Characteristics of Likeable People," clinical psychologist Irene S. Levine writes of the actress, "Her public persona is sweet, attractive, and affable. She has a smile on her face and appears to be better at making and keeping friends than most celebrities. . . ." Levine's nine characteristics pack no surprises: "kind and considerate," "warm, friendly, and outgoing," "vivacious, perky, and engaged in life," "easy to talk to and nonjudgmental," "unpretentious," "interested in others," among them. Fine as far as it goes, but we're still in pleasing-and-agreeable territory. True, likability may help catapult us into the executive suite and public office, but I can't help thinking there's more to being nice.

So, why do we like some people and dislike others? In forming an impression of someone, which personality traits do we respond to favorably and which ones elicit a negative reaction? Over the decades, in an effort to answer such questions, researchers have drawn up laundry lists of traits and asked people to rate each characteristic by how much they would like someone who embodied it. Never mind nine characteristics: some of the lists go on for pages. Norman Anderson at the University of California, San Diego, based a study published in 1968 on a list of 555 traits; a 2002 study by Jean Dumas and his team at Purdue listed 844 "person-descriptive" words, including attitudes and behaviors along with personality traits. Sliced and diced into ever smaller parts, likability is starting to look as if it's as multifarious as we suspect niceness to be. Now the question is: Can we assemble a nice person from likable parts?

The ten most likable traits to emerge from Anderson's study were *sincere, honest, understanding, loyal, truthful, trustworthy, intelligent, dependable, open-minded,* and *thoughtful,* in that order. (Flip them over and you have the ten least likable:

liar, phony, mean, cruel, dishonest, untruthful, obnoxious, mali-cious, dishonorable, and *deceitful.*) The results of the Dumas study placed somewhat more emphasis on the warm and cuddly: *truthful, caring, loyal, honest, friendly, amusing, affec-tionate, trustworthy, lovable,* and *loving.* A 2001 Australian study offered two more cozy choices—*cheerful* and *hospita-ble*—in its top ten. In striking contrast to these results, how-ever, are those of a 1972 German study, in which *tolerant* and *self-critical* emerged as the two most popular traits. Admi-rable characteristics, no doubt, but neither screams "charm-ing personality." Could it be that the Germans, still sensitive to the atrocities of World War II, judged tolerance and the ability to be self-critical necessary as well as desirable—more than their American counterparts did, at any rate?

For the most part, there's been little difference between the sexes in what we find likable in others. But the results of a 1938 study at the University of Illinois provide a window on what men looked for in women before women's lib swept the country. Both the men and the women surveyed prized *intel-ligence* above all in men, but when it came to what the men liked best in women, *beauty* won hands down, with *intelli-gence* a very distant second. (The women found *cheerful* the most likable quality in other women.)

But what are we to make of all these likability lists and stud-ies? Given the variety in the results, it is questionable whether a tossed salad of likable traits would be a reliable guide to likability, never mind niceness. Although each of the qualities in the Nice Survey top ten—*kind*, *helpful*, *courteous*, *considerate*, *compassionate*, *polite*, *gracious*, *attentive*, and *friendly*, with *generous* and *thoughtful* tied for tenth place—appears somewhere on most of the likability lists, there's little correspondence between the lists at the top. So if we can't trust likability to tell us definitively what's nice, where should we look next?

It's possible that our excursion into likability has led us off the path of virtue prematurely. For the most part psychology, along with the rest of the sciences, has assiduously avoided words like *moral* and *virtue* and *values*, but that's starting to change. Social psychologists, cultural anthropologists, even economists, neuroscientists, and evolutionary biologists are looking more closely at morality—at its origins and what it says about us as human beings. This is not religion sneaking in the back door of science, as the evolutionary biologist Richard Dawkins has warned against. The "new synthesis in moral psychology," as University of Virginia psychologist Jonathan Haidt calls it, isn't just looking at right and wrong—"nice versus nasty behaviors"—or "some variant of welfare maximization," but at what purpose morality serves and how everyday moral decisions are made. As the notion of character—specifically, good character—inches back into the picture, the good and the nice are tiptoeing toward a reconciliation of sorts.

One place they come together is in positive psychology. As

the name implies, positive psychology focuses on what's right about human beings rather than what's wrong—what makes us flourish, what makes life worthwhile. With roots in philosophy as well as science, positive psychology has been called "a psychology of wisdom"—a reference to Aristotle's "master" virtue, *praxis,* or practical wisdom. The emphasis is on the inner resources we can draw on to negotiate the business of daily life. As *The Encyclopedia of Positive Psychology* explains, "Scientific psychology is not able to prescribe the morally good life, but it is well equipped to describe the what, how, and why of good character."

With a team of associates, two of positive psychology's leading voices—Christopher Peterson and Martin Seligman, the field's founder—put together a massive compendium, *Character Strengths and Virtues*, that systematically classifies the fundamentals of good character. They call it "a manual of the sanities." Drawing on mountains of psychological research as well as philosophical and spiritual resources from around the globe, Peterson and Seligman arrived at six core virtues—wisdom, courage, humanity, justice, temperance, and transcendence—as the basis of good character. Since virtues per se are hard to pin down, Peterson and Seligman identified twenty-four positive traits or strengths through which the virtues are expressed in everyday life.

If we can search classical psychological literature in vain for the word *nice*, here it is—*niceness*—prominently displayed in *Character Strengths and Virtues* alongside *generosity*, *nurturance*, *care*, *compassion*, and *altruistic love*. In Peterson and Seligman's classification, all these qualities, niceness included, are aspects of kindness, a strength of the virtue of humanity. *Kind*, as we've seen, tops the list of qualities that participants in the Nice Survey associated most closely with *nice*, and *generous* and *compassionate* are not far behind. So we seem to have confirmation from positive psychology that kindness and its cousins are well placed in our definition of *nice*.

Does this mean we could be hardwired to care about others? So it seems. Evolutionary biologists have long held that cooperation is innate: it was essential for ensuring that our early ancestors banded together for survival. But the trait would have died out long ago if it hadn't been useful when our ancestors came off the savannah. Altruism and generosity also appear to be basic drives. Primatologist Frans de Waal found that when a capuchin monkey is given a choice between two colored tokens—one that he can exchange for a slice of apple for himself, or another that he can exchange for two slices (one for himself and one for another monkey), he chooses the token that will benefit them both. Research in people finds that giving to charity lights up the reward centers of the brain—the same areas that fire in response to sex, food, and drugs. Furthermore, being generous means that we're more likely to give again in the future. Now neuroscientists are peering into the brain for evidence of other prosocial behavior. They've already confirmed that we can train ourselves to be more compassionate through meditation, which activates brain regions associated with empathy.

Traditional explanations of why we're generous or kind turn on self-interest. We do things for others with the expectation of receiving something in return—"reciprocal altruism"—or to relieve the discomfort that arises when we see someone suffering, or to avoid other people's criticism or disapproval and look good in their eyes. But research on the effects of oxytocin—the "love" hormone—and the discovery of mirror neurons in the brain are changing our assumptions about how we relate to others. We'll discuss this further in chapter 3, Heaven Is Other People. For now, suffice it to say that there is evidence of neural systems in our brains that fire in response to other people's actions—even their intentions—and are thought to be the basis of empathy.

Positive psychology looks at the disposition to be kind from a perspective other than self-interest. Sometimes we're kind simply because we know it's the right thing to do. Sure, there is a payoff—doing something for others makes us feel good, too. And positive emotions have their own rewards. Barbara Fredrickson, a psychologist at the University of North Carolina at Chapel Hill, says that positive emotions "broaden and build"—broaden our outlook so that we become more open to new ideas and experiences, and build psychological strength, enabling us to experience other people in a more positive and trusting light. Kindness, in short, boosts the happiness of both giver and receiver.

Oddly enough, the pleasure we receive from being kind is one of the reasons that, even as we crave kindness, we sometimes feel ambivalent about it—or so Adam Phillips and Barbara Taylor tell us in their monograph *On Kindness*. We're not as kind as we want to be, and we feel guilty—the authors avoid the word *guilty*, but that's essentially what we feel—that kindness seems to give us so much pleasure. But if we look at it another way, the fact that kindness is mutually beneficial makes it irresistible to all but the most cynical among us.

It's only because of the care we've received that human beings have survived so long, transpersonal psychologist Piero Ferrucci claims; kindness is the "universal remedy" for whatever ails us individually and collectively. Mark Twain called kindness "a language which the deaf can hear and the blind can see." When we asked the Nice Survey participants to recall an incident or experience that struck them as particularly nice, many of the examples they gave were instances in which kindness had been extended to them. Years later, even the simplest gestures were remembered fondly. Donysha Smith, a playwright, recalled receiving a Valentine's Day card from a coworker, with an encouraging note inside. "It was totally unexpected," she said. "It made me feel cared for and considered. I still feel that way." For Chester Burger, a retired management consultant, the roots of a friendship he enjoys to this day were planted by a coworker's "few simple acts of friendliness" at Burger's first job many years ago. While other employees were condescending to the new hire, "one young employee befriended me with courtesy, helpful tips, and minor kindnesses," he said.

Often, the caring actions we remember best are those in which others made personal sacrifices to ensure our comfort and well-being. My niece Meg Morse, now a prep school dean, lived with a Greek family on an exchange program the summer she was sixteen. "I quickly realized that the mother and father had moved out of their bedroom so that I would have the best room in the house," she recalled.

The essence of selfless concern for others lies in what Buddhists call *metta*—loving-kindness—and *karuna,* or compassion. To many, the Dalai Lama is the epitome of kindness and compassion not only because he lives by these qualities himself but also because he inspires them in others. "He strikes me as niceness personified," said Patricia Gift, a book editor who has edited His Holiness's writings and received teachings from him. "He's an advocate for kindness to others as a path to our own happiness. I've experimented with this in my own life and found that it does work. It's such a refreshing counterpoint to the standard American stance of each person for himself or herself."

Compassion is not just a feeling of sympathy, a flutter of the heart, but also a call to action. It makes us want to relieve others' suffering or improve their lives in some way. Mother Teresa ministering to the poor of Calcutta immediately comes to mind, but it could just as easily be the person next door. Lawrence Cann was only twenty-three when he opened a gallery in Charlotte, North Carolina, where the homeless could sell their artwork; he went on to found Street Soccer USA, a nationwide athletic league for homeless people that also provides social services, including helping teens find jobs. As a child, Cann watched his house burn to the ground; he remembered the network of support that rallied around his family, and he wanted to help others who had lost their homes. The Buddha considered generosity—wanting to share what you have and do what you can to help—the basic virtue from which all others followed.

Similar to kindness and compassion is a quality Buddhists call *mudita,* or sympathetic joy. It means being happy for other people's good fortune—a real challenge at times, especially when they have something we want and think we don't have. This sort of open-heartedness is an antidote to the jealousy and envy that can get in the way of appreciation for others. Sincere appreciation is one of Dale Carnegie's "fundamental techniques in handling people" in *How to Win Friends & Influence People*—arguably the most successful self-help book ever written, with well over 15 million copies sold. The language is deceptively simple, but Carnegie's guide is a textbook on being nice. In a section entitled "Six Ways to Make People

Like You," Carnegie suggests: "If we want to make friends, let's put ourselves out to do things for other people—things that require time, energy, unselfishness, and thoughtfulness." In sentiment, if not in those exact words, the Nice Survey participants described what they liked best about the nicest people they know.

Kindness and its cousins generosity, compassion, caring, and altruism are the essence of being human. Just as Blanche DuBois said in *A Streetcar Named Desire*, we depend on the kindness of strangers. And we do it more often than we realize. "Metropolitan Diary," a column in *The New York Times*, regularly includes tales that show the kinder face of a city with a reputation for being cold and uncaring. Yes, New Yorkers have been known to ignore someone lying bleeding on the sidewalk, but those are just the stories that make the evening news. The rest we seldom hear about. Take the miracle on 22nd Street, for example.

Several years ago, out of the blue, Jim and Dylan, two men who live in Manhattan's Chelsea district, began receiving "Dear Santa" letters, all clearly marked with their street address. The letters were written by children, many of them from families that had fallen on hard times and couldn't afford to buy presents for their kids. At first the letters trickled in, a few a year, but by 2010, they were arriving at the rate of forty or so a day. When the total neared four hundred, Jim and Dylan knew they had to do something. But what? They could have taken the letters to the central post office, which every Christmas receives thousands of letters to Santa that it hands out to generous New Yorkers who want to help. But Jim and Dylan were afraid the post office would just stamp the letters "Return to Sender," and they couldn't bear the idea of disappointing the children. So they started giving letters to friends to fulfill the children's wish lists, even posting a request for volunteers on Facebook. There were still hundreds of letters left, but at least it was a start. In a video posted on *The New York Times* City Room blog, Dylan worries that maybe they aren't equipped to handle so many requests. "But that's like saying, 'I can't fix all the world's problems, so I won't fix any,'" Jim counters. That's the difference between them, Dylan tells Jim. "You don't think about it, you just give. That's always been your way. I love that about you."

The two still haven't solved the mystery of how their address got mixed up with Santa's. A reporter from *The New York Times* who investigated hit a dead end. But Jim and Dylan are no longer concerned about why they were chosen. They're busy making plans for next Christmas and how to play Santa to all those kids.

Generosity is such an established—dare I say, expected?—part of friendship that all too often we take it for granted. But the truly generous go beyond the expected, turning up at just the right time with something special. A friend of mine owns an apartment in Paris that he rents out to travelers. After I booked it for a week to celebrate a milestone birthday, he surprised me with a gift: another week—free—at the flat in London he keeps for his personal use. His generosity made a special trip all the more memorable.

Love is another strength of the virtue humanity that Peterson and Seligman describe in their catalogue. Whether romantic, friendly, or familial, caring relationships are fundamental to our happiness and well-being, providing warmth, acceptance, and mutual support. Early parent-child relations are the basis for how secure we feel in relating to others as adults and how readily we form other attachments. It's certainly possible to be nice without being in a committed relationship or being buddy-buddy with family members, but nice people as a rule reach out to others, form emotional bonds, and, when a relationship hits a pothole, make an effort to smooth things out.

Neighborliness can make life worthwhile. Research shows that we are more affected, positively and negatively, by what happens to our neighbors than even to family members. Several of the Nice Survey participants fondly remembered neighborly encounters. Karl Schuman, a graphic artist who lives in a walk-up in New York City, recalled his shock when his new neighbors across the hall "left a nice introductory note and a little gift—a scented candle—at my door." Karl himself is no slouch in the neighborliness department. Once, when I had a bad case of flu, he turned up at my door with a half gallon of ice cream—the only thing I could have eaten in my fevered state. Bob Saxton, a poet who is the editorial director of a London book publisher, described a felicitous meeting with his next-door neighbor shortly after Bob moved into a new flat. "I was gardening and, out of curiosity, climbed a mound to look over the wall into the garden next door. The neighbor was doing the same from the other side. Our faces met, just inches apart, and we had a little chat. He was an interesting old man, an important modernist architect in his time. Two days later, he knocked on my front door, brandishing a bottle of Bailey's Irish Cream liqueur. We sat at my kitchen table drinking Bailey's and talking about social housing."

Together, emotional intelligence and its partner, social intelligence, comprise the third strength of humanity in Peterson and Seligman's classification. Daniel Goleman, whose best-selling book of the same name made "emotional intelligence" a household expression, calls it "the master aptitude." Emotional intelligence is personal—being attuned to and managing our own emotions, and being sensitive to other people and able to form relationships—while social intelligence is interpersonal, including facility in navigating relationships and social situations of all kinds. Just as some people are gifted at intellectual problem solving, there are those who are gifted at grasping the nuances of emotion, motivation, and mood—their own and other people's. Emotional intelligence generally equates to emotional stability, but even a life deficient in love and support can sometimes lead to a profound understanding of others and their needs. Diana, Princess of Wales, is a prime example. She had a tragic childhood and a loveless marriage, yet she was widely regarded as a loving mother and one of the most compassionate people on the planet. Her finely tuned sensibilities gave her a preternatural ability to reach others on an emotional level and empathize with their pain. Indeed, empathy is perhaps the most humanizing of all traits, allowing us to feel a deep connection with people everywhere.

Emotional intelligence and social intelligence are the underpinnings of being nice, the workhorses of the sociable brain. When it comes to connecting with others sensitively, the Nice Survey participants had plenty of examples to share. Although relationships with in-laws are often fraught, literary agent Stephanie Tade described her mother-in-law as "possibly the nicest person in the world. She manages to strike a balance of enormous graciousness, generosity, and thoughtfulness, while maintaining a sense of herself. There isn't a feeling of martyrdom or codependence in her generosity," Tade added. "Every time I see her she wears a piece of jewelry or clothing I gave her as a gift. She doesn't draw attention to it; her acts of generosity seem to come from a more natural place."

Kindness, generosity, compassion, caring—the strengths

of humanity—are characteristics we would expect to find in someone nice. But there are other marks of good character that we also respond to positively in other people—and ideally see value in trying to develop in ourselves. Take temperance, for one. Forget the negative connotations: shades of the Temperance Movement and placard-wielding scolds wagging their fingers at anyone who takes a drink. Peterson and Seligman describe temperance not in moralizing terms but in practical ones: exercising self-control can help us defuse negative emotions that get in the way of achieving our goals.

Acquiring a skill or achieving success at anything requires self-discipline, whether that means resisting a cookie when we're trying to lose weight, curbing the urge to lash out at a colleague when we're rushing to meet a deadline, or studying for the real estate exam when we'd rather play tennis on Wii. One of the most inspiring stories of discipline and determination is that of Hugh McDonald, who proved that with diligence it's never too late to realize a childhood dream. A commuter bus driver, McDonald rose every morning before dawn at his home in Pennsylvania to put in twelve- and fourteen-hour days plying the route between Philadelphia and New York City. One day, while walking through the Times Square subway station, he heard someone playing Bach on a cello. McDonald was transfixed. As a child growing up in a Bronx housing project, he had yearned to learn an instrument but his parents said no. At age fifty-one, he decided to take the plunge. He rented a cello, picked a music school out of the phone book—it happened to be located at Carnegie Hall—and practiced diligently in the back of his bus during breaks. McDonald's dedication earned him a chair in a community orchestra, and then he began nursing a new dream: playing cello in a symphony orchestra.

Our own ambitions may take a very different form, but any accomplishment involves self-discipline of some sort. If the connection between being nice and mastering the cello still isn't clear, consider how much you admire someone who has become proficient at something or surmounted an obstacle or attained an important goal—or even just developed a modicum of self-control. Hollywood star Drew Barrymore certainly knows what it's like to overcome challenges through hard work. A child star at seven—who could forget her in *E.T.: The Extra-Terrestrial*?—she was already drinking, drugging, and clubbing as a preteen, and entered her first rehab at thirteen. Living on her own by age fifteen, she continued to party hard while playing vamps onscreen and posing nude for *Interview* and *Playboy*. Then, with the help of people like Steven Spielberg, her *E.T.* director, she began to turn her life around. At twenty, she formed a production company, Flower Films, and in the years since she has not only straightened up her private life but also become a force in Hollywood, producing and starring in movies with strong roles for women. A savvy businesswoman, Barrymore parlayed her fresh-faced beauty into lucrative contracts as the face of Cover Girl makeup and Gucci jewelry. Off camera, she has put her energy behind such causes as the United Nations World Food Programme, where she serves as an ambassador against hunger.

Barrymore's transformation is a dramatic example of temperance in action—a testament to the benefits of self-discipline and restraint. What can we infer from temperance? For one thing, that the person in question can set priorities and see things through, and therefore, in all likelihood, will be a reliable coworker, friend, or lover. (*Trustworthy* and *dependable*—high on some likability lists—come to mind.)

Other aspects of temperance call for a different sort of restraint. Take forgiveness. There isn't a person alive who hasn't been wronged and, I dare say, had at least a passing desire for revenge. The trouble with resentment and its uglier cousin, hatred, is that they're so damaging, not least to the person who harbors the grudge. Forgiveness is for victim and perpetrator alike. Until we become willing to forgive, we will never rid ourselves of the one who did us wrong. And if it's someone else's forgiveness we're seeking for something we've done, the faster we can make amends, the sooner our shame and guilt will be lifted. Sometimes direct amends aren't possible, but becoming willing to right a wrong and making an effort in that direction are key aspects of the transaction.

In the foreword to *Forgiveness: A Time to Love and a Time to Hate*, the companion book to a documentary film by Helen

....

"What do you prefer, to die twice or to forgive and live?"

....

Whitney, the Dalai Lama writes: "Forgiveness is not a question of forgetting the wrong done; if you've forgotten what was done, there is nothing to forgive. Forgiveness involves refusing to allow yourself to give in to anger and the desire for revenge. This is the way forgiveness ultimately brings peace."

One of the people Whitney interviewed for the film is a Rwandan pastor who witnessed the horrific genocide in his country and has worked tirelessly for unity and reconciliation ever since. When someone protested that forgiving the killers would be desecrating the memory of the victims, the pastor countered: "What do you prefer, to die twice or to forgive and live?"

The ability to forgive is a hallmark of nice people, as is the humility to seek forgiveness from others. Humility, or modesty, is another strength associated with temperance that endears us to others and earns their respect. "This character strength is a quiet one," Peterson and Seligman write. "Those who are modest let their accomplishments speak for themselves." We value humility, although, as Peterson and Seligman point out, we value it "if not always in ourselves then certainly in others." In this age of relentless self-promotion, it's refreshing to find people who aren't loudly crowing about how smart/clever/funny/talented/good-looking they are, or drawing attention to themselves in some other way. Once, in the days when Robert Redford was number one at the box office, I happened to walk up Fifth Avenue behind him as he threaded his way through the Saturday tourist crowds. A poster for his latest film was plastered on every lamppost we passed, but amazingly, no one even looked at Redford. He had dialed down the charisma and become just another guy walking up Fifth Avenue on a Saturday afternoon.

Yet another trait associated with temperance is prudence, and if it sounds a little uptight and unexciting, Peterson and Seligman point out another, sexier side: smart thinking. This is Kate Middleton walking the tightrope of discretion in the sure knowledge that any whiff of scandal would quash her chances of marrying Prince William. (Her opposite number is Sarah Ferguson, the Duchess of York, who was caught trying to peddle access to her ex-husband, Prince Andrew—an imprudent move, if ever there was one.) People die—or kill their marriages, or careers, or reputations, or all of the above—as a result of taking foolish chances. Think of the politician John Edwards, who lost it all, or Bill Clinton, who very nearly did. As much as we may dislike a Goody Two-shoes, we are drawn to someone with balance and restraint, who can be counted on not to do or say something inappropriate or stupid.

Wisdom is another core virtue that at first may be difficult to connect with *nice*. But like the other strengths we've discussed, those associated with wisdom aim at character building. Creativity and original thinking, curiosity and openness to experience, love of learning—when we meet people who embody any of these qualities, what's not to like? The strengths of wisdom, Peterson and Seligman tell us, involve gaining and using knowledge in vital, often unexpected ways. My mother dropped out of college and married young, but she remained a passionate learner throughout her life. A voracious and wide-ranging reader, she passed on her thirst for knowledge as if she were bequeathing us the family fortune— which she was. To this day, I strive to master her gift of "bibliothérapie"—finding just the right book to stimulate conversation or lift a blue mood.

Creativity isn't just for artists; it can ratchet up the ordinary, making an adventure out of the most routine activity. When I was young, a friend and I hired ourselves out to wash dishes after parties. Our best clients were a couple who had been in the foreign service and often entertained visitors from abroad. The food was always—to our palates—exotic, and there was usually a film or slide lecture on a faraway place or an abstruse topic. To us, the hosts weren't just nice, they were magical, opening up the world to two young, impressionable girls.

One of the most colorful exemplars of wisdom was the charismatic, bongo-playing, Nobel Prize–winning theoretical physicist Richard Feynman. Infinitely curious, Feynman saw life as a never-ending adventure and himself as an explorer. "My interest in science is simply to find out about the world," he told a filmmaker who was shooting a documentary about his life. A polymath and a genius in the true sense of the word—a person with a "great and original creative ability"—Feynman was also a prankster. On a lark, he and a friend cooked up a plan to travel to Tannu Tuva, a remote province in central Siberia that was then still part of the Soviet Union. For ten years they pursued the dream, learning Tuvan from a Mongolian-Tuvan phrase book so they could correspond with the governor, mastering (in a fashion) Tuvan throat singing from an ethnographer's recording, even persuading a California art museum to mount an exhibit of Tuvan artifacts—all in an effort to secure visas to visit the remote spot. The visas finally came through—five days after Feynman's death. It hardly mattered. In his last interview, Feynman said that what delighted him about the whole project was "the fun of having an adventure of going to a land we'd never heard of." Wisdom, as Feynman's life so clearly illustrates, is the virtue of those who never stop turning over rocks to find out what lies beneath.

When we think of courage, another of the core virtues described in *Character Strengths and Virtues*, we immediately think of bravery: the Navy Seals who took down Osama bin Laden; the firefighters who rushed into the World Trade Center towers on 9/11. But the virtue of courage extends beyond physical daring, Peterson and Seligman tell us. We don't need to serve on the front lines or save a child from drowning to be courageous: just "soldiering through" a difficult time is a show of valor.

Courage involves strength of will: persistence—often against the odds—as well as industriousness, integrity, and a zest for life. This is Rosa Parks, the African-American southerner whose refusal to give up her seat on the bus to a white passenger was a defining moment in the Civil Rights Movement. Or Erin Brockovich and whistleblowers like her, who dare to speak out against pollution or corruption, saving whole communities in the process. But there is courage as well in the anonymous hotel maid who with hard work and perseverance puts her three kids through college, or the plucky septuagenarian who backpacks across South America. Carrying on in the face of illness or loss is brave, as is taking the high road when a shortcut would be easier. Often courage is simply standing up to our fears.

How does all this relate to being nice? "Courage is something we want for ourselves in gluttonous portions and adore in others without qualification," science journalist Natalie Angier once observed. I think of an obituary I read not long ago. The deceased was a forty-year-old lawyer, volunteer, and mother of two who had survived a heart transplant and become an advocate for organ donation before she died. "Emily demonstrated to all who knew and loved her that she would live life to the fullest with no regrets," her obituary reads. "Empathy, inquisitiveness, courage, and determination defined her daily life." Don't you wish you had known her? I do. *Nice* doesn't describe her by half.

Everyone loves a hero. "We love heroes because of what they offer us—hope for a better world," Scott Allison, a social psychologist at the University of Richmond, told *USA Today*. "We have a need for heroes because we have a need to be challenged." Challenging us all to be heroes is the purpose of the Heroic Imagination Project launched by Philip Zimbardo, a Stanford University psychology professor emeritus. "Heroes are really the soul of a nation," Zimbardo said. "They represent what is best in human nature."

Zimbardo reminds us that heroes are simply ordinary people who do something extraordinary. All of New York City—indeed the nation—was captivated by the valor of the "Subway Samaritan," Wesley Autrey. A fifty-one-year-old construction worker and Navy veteran, he leapt onto the subway tracks to save a young man who had had a seizure and stumbled off the platform into the path of an oncoming train. Afterward, Autrey was showered with honors by the city, and lauded for his bravery by the White House. But he brushed aside any talk of heroism. "I just saw someone who needed help. I did what I felt was right," he told *The New York Times*. Autrey credited his experience on construction sites with allowing him to correctly judge that if he flattened himself on top of the victim in the trough between the tracks, there would be just enough room for the train to pass safely overhead. The only mark on either man was a streak of grease on Autrey's cap.

Autrey and others like him may deflect attention away from their heroic deeds, but their actions can have far-reaching effects. Seeing someone do a good deed or something heroic—even just hearing about it—engenders a feeling that psychologist Jonathan Haidt calls "elevation." We stand up taller, our chests swell, we're suffused with warm feelings, maybe even moved to tears. What's more, those feelings make us want to do something worthwhile ourselves. One of Haidt's research subjects related this example: She was in a carload of people driving home from volunteering at the Salvation Army. It had been snowing heavily, and as the car passed an elderly woman shoveling her driveway, one of the passengers asked the driver to stop. He then jumped out of the car, ran over to the woman, and offered to shovel for her. When the other passengers saw this, they experienced a surge of positive emotion. "I felt like jumping out of the car and hugging this guy. I felt like singing and running, or skipping and laughing," the storyteller recalled. "I felt like saying nice things about people. Writing a beautiful poem or love song. Playing in the snow like a child."

Elevation is powerful. The moral goodness of others arouses good feelings in us. And we like people who make us feel good. When those warm feelings, in turn, make us want to do things for others, the goodness keeps spreading. Everyone seems nicer, and every encounter is bathed in niceness.

Which brings us to another virtue Peterson and Seligman identified: transcendence. The word smacks of religiosity but the meaning here is broader. Transcendence refers to a connection with something larger than oneself. Gratitude is one of the associated strengths. It's hardly surprising that we find grateful people nice—or that feeling grateful makes us nicer. "Gratitude is a gift, gratitude is sharing, gratitude is love: it is a joy accompanied by the idea of its cause," wrote the French philosopher André Comte-Sponville, "when the cause is another person's generosity, or courage, or love." Like elevation, gratitude is expansive, opening the heart. "Gratitude can never diminish others," Peterson and Seligman explain. "Even the most awkward Academy Award acceptance speech or muttered 'thank you' by a manly man initiates an episode that elevates participants and onlookers."

Gratitude marries the good and the nice. It is part of every spiritual tradition, and people who are plugged in spiritually often find ways to acknowledge appreciation for their lives, their health, their loved ones, their well-being. Many people say grace before meals. There is a verse chanted before meals at Dai Bosatsu Kongo-ji, a Zen monastery in upstate New York, that invites deeper reflection than the usual dinnertime prayer tossed off by rote. It acknowledges that whatever we receive in life involves the generosity of untold others:

First, let us reflect on our own work and the effort of those
who brought us this food.
Secondly, let us be aware of the quality of our deeds as we
receive this meal.
Thirdly, what is most essential is the practice of
mindfulness, which helps us transcend greed, anger,
and delusion.
Fourthly, we appreciate this food which sustains the good
health of our body and mind.
Fifthly, in order to continue our practice for all beings, we
accept this offering.

In this age of instant messaging, a handwritten thank-you
note is precious, a confirmation of the writer's appreciation—
or good manners, at the very least. Receiving it, we feel grateful in return—for the note writer's time and effort in finding
nice stationery, composing a thoughtful sentiment, and posting the letter. Nice people acknowledge gifts and favors.
Ingratitude chafes. Failing to express appreciation has soured
many a relationship.

Hope is another strength we find nice in those who embody
it. "The thing with feathers," as the poet Emily Dickinson
famously put it, hope "keeps us warm" through thick and
thin. When Pandora let the evils out of the box, only hope
remained. It's what buoys us up and keeps us going, psychologist Barbara Fredrickson observed: "With hope, we become

energized to do as much as we can to make a good life for
ourselves and for others."

Hope is the currency of optimistic people. We gravitate to
optimists, drawn by their confidence that things will work
out and that others are behind them. We're suspicious of *naïve*
optimists—the wide-eyed Candides of the world who think
everything is peachy-keen and getting better by the minute.
But pessimistic Eeyore, eating thistles in the yard, won't win
many popularity contests either. Research shows that although pessimists have a better grounding in present reality, optimists are happier and better liked. They look to the
future and see its promise. The charm of optimists is perfectly
summed up in the famous line, often misattributed to Robert Kennedy, from George Bernard Shaw's play *Back to Methuselah*: "You see things; and you say, 'Why?' But I dream
things that never were; and I say, 'Why not?'"

Humor is another strength of transcendence that is a great
attractor. Humor in this context isn't the comic—jokes or
stand-up routines or punking the neighbors—but playfulness,
a perspective on life that can see the lighter side even in the
midst of adversity. Samuel Clemens, aka Mark Twain, is Peterson and Seligman's exemplar of this strength. It may not be
evident from reading *Tom Sawyer* or *Huckleberry Finn* or

Hope is the currency of optimistic people.

Twain's journals of his travels, but his life had its share of hardship. His wife's early death left him a single father; he suffered chronic money worries, including bankruptcy. Humor, Twain said, was what made it all bearable.

Freud viewed humor as a psychic release valve—a safe way to express pent-up aggression and sexual desire. Often humor comes out of seeing incongruities; the logic of humor lies in catastrophe theory—an abrupt switch in perspective that makes us view something in an unexpected way, so we laugh. Humor brings us together in shared amusement. We love people who make us laugh; it can be the glue that holds a relationship together. Many people cite humor as what drew them to their spouse or romantic partner and keeps them hanging in. Joking relationships can be among the most pleasant and enduring. For years, my father played doubles tennis with the same men, and, on or off the court, their affectionate kidding was a noticeable bond.

The sixth of the core virtues Peterson and Seligman write about is justice. They describe it as the virtue of community life, with strengths related to teamwork, loyalty, fairness, leadership, and social responsibility. Linking justice to *nice* seems like a stretch. But when you consider Nelson Mandela's secrets of leadership—a lifetime of wisdom distilled for *Time* magazine on the occasion of his ninetieth birthday—the connection between leadership and niceness is suddenly vivid and real. "Courage is not the absence of fear—it's inspiring others to move beyond it," is Mandela's rule number one. "Lead from the back—and let others believe they are in front" is another rule. And in a twist on "keep your friends close, your enemies closer," there is this: "Know your enemy—and learn about his favorite sport." Mandela is an exemplar of many, if not most of the twenty-four strengths of positive psychology, and his desire to humanize those who opposed him was more than just strategic. While in prison on Robben Island, Mandela, who had trained as a lawyer, flabbergasted his jailers—the worst apartheid thugs—by helping them with legal issues. Mandela was no Christ turning the other cheek, however: Richard Stengel, who wrote the *Time* cover story, tells us that Mandela "is not and never has been introspective." Mandela's explanation? In prison, he said, he matured.

A good leader can inspire us—even bring out the best in us—but still not be someone we want to take home and introduce to the family. That said, there are studies showing that we vote—indeed, make most decisions—first with our hearts and then with our heads. We feel the emotion, then marshal the reasons. An appealing personality is a vote-getter, predisposing us to think the candidate is nice, competent, smart, and more. John Kerry's lack of warmth and social ease—his public face—probably cost him the 2004 presidential election; the more gregarious and outgoing George W. Bush emerged the winner.

Loyalty and fairness, two other strengths of justice, are also qualities we might add to the basket of traits we consider nice. Mohandas Gandhi is Peterson and Seligman's exemplar of fairness: "someone who successfully developed his moral reasoning, in both the justice and the care senses of that term." Few of us can identify with Gandhi's struggles. But we don't have to lead a national freedom movement or campaign for the disenfranchised to understand what it is to be fair. There are many levels to fairness, and, at its simplest, it is one of the most commonsensical traits—the antidote to the favoritism that pervades every area of life, down to which child gets the bigger slice of cake. We like people who are even-handed and mistrust those who aren't. Perhaps this strength relates to *nice* most clearly when we find it absent in someone.

And then there is loyalty. Peterson and Seligman include it as an aspect of good citizenship. Loyalty to country or church or point of view doesn't have much to do with being nice, perhaps—we might admire or respect someone for her dedication, but it probably wouldn't be the first or second thing about her personality we would find attractive. If we consider someone nice because she's a devout Catholic or an ardent supporter of the ASPCA, it's very likely because she mirrors something we value highly in ourselves, such as our own commitment to the church or our love of animals.

But there are other aspects of loyalty than devotion to country or cause, and it's these that concern us most in the search for *nice*. Personal loyalty—fidelity to loved ones and friends—is a big part of being nice. We want the people we care about to keep their promises to us and stick by us, just as we feel a duty to be trustworthy and present for them. "We learn to be faithful to love received," André Comte-Sponville writes, "to a show of trust, to a certain standard. . . ."

Laid out like this, virtues and strengths can seem daunting. Who could possibly claim all the qualities Peterson and Seligman describe in *Character Strengths and Virtues*? Rest assured, they assume nothing of the sort. These traits, if not universal, are "ubiquitously recognized and valued," state Peterson and Seligman, who profess to being "comfortable in saying that someone is of good character if he or she displays but one or two strengths within a virtue group."

But which ones? you might ask. Clearly the strengths aren't interchangeable—so equal in weight that which one or two we pick makes no difference to our moral balance. What happens if circumstances call for a strength we don't possess—can we still claim to be of good character? And then there's Peterson and Seligman's suggestion that character development consists of identifying the strengths we already possess and enhancing them further. Is that really the most effective strategy? Isn't it a bit like suggesting that a weightlifter whose legs are weak should compensate by pumping up his already well-developed pecs? It may be unrealistic to think we could develop all twenty-four strengths, but I wonder if we shouldn't at least try to expand our repertoire. How can we be of good character if our inner being is so lopsided? I may be humble to a fault and forgiveness personified, but if I've never met a rule I wouldn't flout or a chance I wouldn't take, what sort of person am I? And what if I show a strength in some situations but not in others—can I still claim it as my own? Peterson and Seligman allow for such deviations. So if I'm a nurse, it makes sense to show kindness in one way at the hospital—a little tough love, say, to get my patient up and walking—but to be gentler at home when one of my children breaks an arm. But there can be a downside to relative virtue. Maybe I'm generous only when it suits me, and oblivious to other situations in which a need is clear. If I'm a model of self-control most of the time but I fly off the handle when anyone disciplines my dog, will I automatically be blackballed by the temperance club?

Questions about virtue have fueled debates for centuries. There are those who see character as stable and the virtues as "robust"—you either display a virtue across the board or you can't lay claim to it at all. Tell a white lie out of kindness and you can strike integrity off the list. At the other extreme are those who argue that virtues are situational, called forth only by the circumstances of the moment. But here, too, there's a problem. What if I do something that's virtuous on the face of it, but the underlying motivation is all wrong? A Mafia don might shower presents on the family, but if he financed his largesse from his rackets, surely that would cancel out any credit for being generous? Look at it another way: would you want him at your dinner table? *Dishonest* is the least likable trait of the 844 on Dumas's list.

In short, is there some sort of algorithm for calculating how many traits it takes to be virtuous, and how many—and which ones—to be nice? I might enjoy and respect a friend for his lively mind but find his political views repellant and therefore feel conflicted about spending time with him. Research shows that "frenemies," friends we feel ambivalent about, are more stressful to be around than people we outright dislike. We don't have any expectations of the latter but we hold out hope that *this* time our frenemy will come through for us. Each of us has a different threshold of tolerance for the character and behavior of others. Arguments about politics may be catnip to you—the more contentious, the better—while they tie my stomach in knots. Someone may be a first-class procrastinator, but unless what he's holding hostage is my tax return or the yearly budget, I won't be all that upset. But you, meanwhile, might already have erased his name from your address book.

Which brings us to what may be the most salient fact in our investigation of nice. Ultimately our assessment of other people and behavior may have little to do with traits. After all, we don't run around with lists of the personal qualities we like and, when we meet people, tick off how many of our criteria they meet. (Well, maybe we do that on those online dating sites that match up potential partners on the basis of everything from eye-color preference to income and spiritual values.) But the point is, is someone nice simply because she has *x* number of nice traits? After all, we are not pointillist paintings made of a million little dots that only when viewed at a distance form a pleasing and coherent image. When we meet someone, we experience the whole—a gestalt, if you will. As the pioneering social psychologist Solomon Asch described it, "We look at a person and immediately a certain impression of his character forms itself in us. A glance, a few spoken words, are sufficient to tell us a story about a highly complex matter. We know that such impressions form with remarkable rapidity and ease. Subsequent observation may enrich or upset our first view, but we can no more prevent its rapid growth than we can avoid perceiving a given visual object or hearing a melody."

Asch contended that, over time, our impression of someone is likely to change. (As we'll see in chapter 5, Love, Love Me Do, others more recently have argued that first impressions are hard to shake.) Either way, any change in our perceptions of someone isn't simply a function of the other person revealing himself to us: yes, the observed person changes but so also does the observer. Our impression of someone is based not only on the qualities and behavior we see in him but also on what we bring to the encounter. Our own moods and emotions, prejudices and preconceptions, fears and doubts, color the way we see others. Looking for our model nice person is, in a sense, a fool's errand. We don't live in a world of the hypothetical or ideal, and who and what we find nice is grounded in real situations with real individuals. Even the kindest, most caring person has bad days. And if I'm the one in a bad mood, your warmth and gregariousness may grate on me like a file. Then, too, someone may be super-nice at work but at home, a distant husband and an ogre of a father.

Let's look again at the Subway Samaritan, Wesley Autrey. We know he's brave and quick-thinking and seems to have a well-developed sense of compassion. But is he nice? What's he like at home? Is he a caring friend, an attentive father? When he jumped onto the tracks, he left his two little daughters standing on the platform. What if he had been hurt—or worse yet, killed? Would we still find him courageous and self-less, or call him irresponsible and reckless? Autrey's bravery and humility created a "halo effect": from those positive qualities we infer all kinds of things about him—that he's kind, loving, generous, resourceful, and so on. We even give him the benefit of the doubt about leaving his daughters. After all, a bystander kept them safe until he was back on the platform. But we can't really know if Autrey is affable or interesting or funny or whatever else we consider nice until we spend some time with him. *Nice* has an elastic quality, expanding and contracting as a result of so many factors, not least the mood of the person who's doing the evaluating.

When we like people, we tend to see them as more attractive and make other positive assumptions about them. "Such a phenomenon could best be described as a deduction from an implicit personality theory holding that 'nice people tend to have nice attributes and less nice people have less nice attributes,'" explain Richard Nisbett and Timothy DeCamp Wilson, researchers at the University of Michigan. But if all this suggests that *everything* is in the eye of the beholder, that assumption would be wrong as well. Some people seem to be intrinsically nice. A former executive producer for the NBC show *Today* said of Ann Curry, one of the hosts, "She is as good and caring off-air as she appears to be on-air. That is a rare and special quality."

Curry's life seems to be informed by compassion. She has bungee-jumped off a bridge for charity, and on more than one occasion has grown her hair long so she could cut it off and donate it to an organization that makes wigs for children who've lost their hair to cancer or alopecia. Curry's coverage has put a human face on some of the most harrowing and tragic situations of our time—Kosovo, Darfur, and Sudan among them. Her mission, she has said, is to be a witness to human suffering. "As a child when I learned that there were people who risked their own lives and even the lives of their children, their families, to save Jews during the Holocaust, it was a profound moment for me," she told a reporter. "It made me question whether I am the kind of human being who would take such risks." No one doubts she is.

A positive trait or strength doesn't necessarily make us nice just because we possess it. How we express it in the world is the issue. Take curiosity, for example. Is it motivated by a genuine interest in others and getting to know them better— or a desire to probe people's secrets and get the goods on them for your own selfish ends? It's not hard to guess which of those two we would be more likely to find nice. We like people who show an interest in us—so long as their interest isn't salacious or predatory. Research also shows we tend to like people who are similar to us: they mirror back to us our best qualities. (And our worst, but we tend to ignore those.) Of course, we also may project onto others qualities we like in ourselves: are you nice because I see my own niceness in you? When it comes to first impressions, narcissists make a better showing than those without the neurotic need to seduce. But although a narcissist may seem nice at first, inevitably once we come closer and the veil is lifted, the narcissist's self-centeredness makes him less attractive to us.

So how do we recognize the genuinely nice among us? Is there a secret to becoming genuinely nice ourselves? If niceness consisted merely of embodying a few chosen strengths and virtues, then cultivating it would be as straightforward as ordering camping equipment from the L.L. Bean catalog. And choosing nice friends and intimate partners would be a simple matter of applying the kind of "moral algebra" Benjamin Franklin recommended to his nephew: list their bad points on one side, good on the other, see which ones cancel each other out, then decide on the basis of what remains. Unfortunately, however, *nice* isn't quite so formulaic, and character formation doesn't consist of following a recipe with a standard set of ingredients. Each of us embodies our own complement of virtues, strengths, and attitudes—good and bad—that we live out in a singular way.

Webster's definition of *nice* is "a generalized term of approval meaning variously (a) agreeable; pleasant; delightful; (b) attractive; pretty; (c) courteous and considerate; (d) conforming to approved social standards; respectable; (e) in good taste; (f) good; excellent." We've already gone there and beyond, opening up the definition to include other aspects of character. In the process, we've discovered that being nice is not a solo endeavor. "Personal identity" is almost a misnomer: while each of us comes with a set of genes for the physical body and even personality traits, our sense of self develops out of our relationships with family, friends, the community, and, some would say, God or a spiritual power, and the natural world.

Once we get to the social side of being nice, the story lies in those famous words of E. M. Forster: "Only connect!"

Chapter Three

Heaven Is Other People

There's no need for red-hot pokers," Jean-Paul Sartre wrote in the play *No Exit*. "Hell is—other people." He didn't mean to imply that relationships are impossible, he later explained. In fact, we only know ourselves through others, he said: "Into whatever I say about myself someone else's judgment always enters." The oft-quoted line "Hell is other people," far from a condemnation of society, merely underscores how important other people are to us. Not that there aren't some days we might not take Sartre's line at face value: who hasn't found socializing exhausting at times or, on a bad day, had less than charitable thoughts about humanity? But the mood always passes. We can't imagine life without other people. Far from hell, they are our heaven on earth.

We're members of a raucous, sometimes fractious, often harmonious chorus.

Up to now we've been looking at niceness from the standpoint of the individual: how I, with a personality that's a grab bag of traits, attitudes, capabilities, and behaviors, regard you with your personality, similarly constructed. As it happens, of course, we never see one another broken down into constituent parts, like a car disassembled for repairs on the floor of a garage. We perceive one another whole, as living, breathing, thinking, emoting beings. And as much as we celebrate individuality, we don't exist in isolation in the day-to-day world. Life is a social affair, and nearly every action is an interaction. Social psychologist Nicholas Emler found that on average we spend 80 percent of our waking hours with other people, between six and twelve of those hours in conversation. (Your ratio may be different—mine certainly is—but you get the picture.) We may think we're performing a solo, but in reality we're members of a raucous, sometimes fractious, often harmonious chorus.

The Social Animal, Social Intelligence, The Social Brain, The Moral Animal—book titles like these tell the story. Even if you spend all your waking hours online, in the virtual world you are still a creature of community. We humans evolved big brains so we could navigate our ever-changing social environment, a world full of people and complex interrelation-ships. Large chunks of the brain are devoted to the so-called "moral" emotions—anger, guilt, embarrassment, compassion, and the like—which are called up when we interact with oth-ers. "We are wired to connect," Daniel Goleman writes in *Social Intelligence*, a follow-up to his best seller *Emotional Intelligence*. The social circuits in the brain "seem to be always 'on,' ever ready to act," he explains.

So what are the skills that allow us to get along well with others? What do we need to know to become nice people? If we're built to connect, what's the connection—how do we blossom and become our best selves in the company of others?

There is much more to being nice than minding your man-ners, staying upbeat, and once in a while extending a helping hand. Kindness and its cousins generosity, compassion, car-ing, and love—so critical to our health and well-being—are both the glue and the lubricant of social life, and they're deeply imbedded in our brains. You know that irritating friend of yours who claims she has ESP and can tell what you're thinking—and what you're about to do before you do it? Guess what: she may be right. What may surprise you even more, perhaps, is that you have the same intuitive sense about her; you just may not recognize it as such. And then there's the friend who seems to be hypersensitive to your emotional weather in a Bill Clinton, I-feel-your-pain sort of way. What's *his* story?

Social circuitry again. Our social environment isn't just a pleasant or convenient place to hang out. What goes on there literally reshapes our brains and, in so doing, remakes our world. Throughout our lives, we are being nudged into becoming the individuals we are today by our interactions with the people around us. Cornelia Bargmann, a Rockefeller University professor who studies genetic control of social behavior, has explained it like this: "From the moment of our birth, the most important aspect of our life is our ability to predict and affect the behavior of others."

It begins with looking into the faces of our caregivers. Mom smiles at baby, baby smiles back, positive emotion flooding his brain as it picks up happy signals from Mom's brain. And the emotional communication doesn't just go one way. When baby frowns, Mom frowns, echoing his distress. The social circuitry in our brains resonates with other people's emotions. Quite literally, we feel what they feel. "All emotions are social," observed neuropsychologist Richard Davidson, director of the Laboratory for Affective Neuroscience at the University of Wisconsin. "You can't separate the cause of emotion from the world of relationships—our social interactions are what drive our emotions."

So how does that work? How is it that we feel what others are feeling—their suffering and their joy? What is the source of the "emotional contagion" that makes my mood spread to you—and yours to me—like a fast-moving flu? The answers, researchers are finding, lie in special brain cells known as mirror neurons. Mirror neuron systems are thought to be the underpinning of interpersonal relations and the source of empathy—the ability to feel what others are feeling and see things from their perspective, along with a desire to take compassionate action to relieve their suffering.

Watching someone do something—reach for a chocolate bar, let's say—fires up circuitry in the brain to mimic the action. I don't even have to actually follow through and grab the chocolate bar myself, but my brain experiences the same urge as the chocolate-eater. Imagine the ramifications of this ability to mirror one another's emotions and intentions—not just those of our nearest and dearest but of everyone around us. When a stranger across the room picks up her crying baby to soothe it, I am both the infant in distress and the worried mother. What a relief I feel when she cuddles the infant and her soft cooing and gentle touch calm him. As mother and child relax, the tension in *my* stomach releases. Now all is well for the three of us. Obviously, the bond between mother and child is special and especially strong, but all of us have the capacity to identify with—and soothe—someone in distress. Thinking of family, friends, and colleagues—even political leaders—we all know a few whose calm demeanor can bring a roomful of people into harmony, or at least get them to lay down their swords and talk to one another.

This ability to understand and experience others' emotional states and intuit their intentions is the crux of human communication, but mirror neurons were first discovered by scientists working with monkeys. Like many great discoveries, this one was serendipitous. Researchers in Giacomo Rizzolatti's lab at the University of Parma were mapping a part of the brain involved in planning and executing movement. Their research partners were macaque monkeys with electrodes planted in their brains. When a monkey grasped an object, the relevant area of his brain lit up, and a monitor hooked up to the electrodes made a buzzing sound. There are various stories about what happened next. In one version, a lab monkey was sitting quietly waiting for the next procedure when a researcher reached for something, and simultaneously the monkey's monitor buzzed. In other versions, a researcher was eating an ice cream cone or, alternatively, cracking open a peanut when the monkey's monitor sounded. But regardless of how it all started, in subsequent trials the researchers found that the same cells in the monkey's brain that fired when he grasped an object fired when he merely saw or heard someone else doing the same thing. Later research uncovered mirror neuron systems in humans that give us direct access to other people's emotions and intentions.

Not everyone in the scientific community is convinced that mirror neurons exist in humans—or that they function as researchers have suggested. Even among believers, there is still disagreement about how extensive mirror neuron systems are and how much of our behavior they affect. But the possibility that we are so closely bound to one another is not only exciting—we're wired to really "get" one another!—it also carries a responsibility. Think about it. You have no doubt experienced times when someone else's mood—happy, sad, frightened, upset—affected you. But you may not have realized just how strong the effect was—how contagious emotions are. When I'm friendly and respectful to you, you feel good, so you are more likely to treat the next people you meet with the same regard. But if the mood you caught from me is a negative one, the ripple effect will not be so pleasant. It doesn't take a genius to figure out how broad our emotional reach can be. Quite literally, then, we have a civic duty to be nice to one another. "Without deep reflection one knows from daily life that one exists for other people," Albert Einstein allegedly said. Whether or not those were his words, the sentiment rings true. It may not be important to know which areas of the brain light up when we are feeling kind or compassionate—or out of sorts. But realizing our brain-to-brain connection is an incentive to be more mindful of our thoughts and emotions as well as our actions.

Mirroring is the basis for empathy, allowing us to understand others' suffering from the inside out. It used to be thought that to have a sense of others' pain, we had to first observe their behavior and from that infer their emotional state. Now we know that perception and emotion come first; then cognition kicks in. The emotional system that reads other people is a direct path from your brain to mine. (Dan Goleman calls it "neural WiFi.") I don't need to consciously deduce what you're feeling; I experience it in my body, although other brain cells inhibit me from acting out your intentions.

Some people seem to be especially attuned to others' suffering. One of the Nice Survey participants, magazine managing editor Rachel Hiles, related a vivid example of empathy and fellow feeling:

> My oldest friend, David, had an older brother—he was twenty-two at the time—who was dying of cancer. At the same time, my elderly grandmother was hospitalized after falling in her apartment. David's father found out that she was ill and sent a huge bouquet of beautiful flowers to her hospital room. I was so amazed that despite his own immense troubles—his wife had died of cancer several years before and now he was watching his son go down the same path—David's father took the time to think of my sick grandma, a woman he had met only a handful of times, and send something he knew would bring her joy.

This is a perfect demonstration of the feedback loop of empathy and kindness. We can imagine David's father, his brain in sync with that of his dying son, experiencing similar emotional resonance with Rachel's ailing grandmother. The joy he brought to the elderly lady would cycle back to him—generosity lights up the reward or pleasure centers of the brain—even as the positive feelings spread in ever-widening circles to Rachel and others who heard about his thoughtful gesture. Dacher Keltner, a psychology professor at the University of California, Berkeley, studies just this sort of transaction as director of the Greater Good Science Center. When people feel compassion for others, he explained, "this emotion is reflected in very real physiological changes: their heart rate goes down from baseline levels, which prepares them not to fight or flee, but to approach and soothe."

Clearly being nice isn't just a pleasant add-on, something that makes life a little easier or better for us and, perhaps, for those around us. Getting along with other people, no matter how fleeting the encounter, and establishing healthy and caring relationships are essential to being human, and the substrate of being nice. It hardly matters if I sob at the sight of earthquake victims in Haiti if I can't be bothered to check on my aging neighbor. And knowing that any negativity I'm feeling is directly transmitted to others, whether they like it or not, prompts me to consider how to modify my thinking and behavior to make sure that their day, as well as mine, runs smoothly.

"Flourishing" or well-being—*eudaimonia* to the ancient Greeks—is the core concept in positive psychology and the goal of life. Martin E. P. Seligman, one of the founders of the positive psychology movement, has come up with an acronym, PERMA, that stands for the five factors that define flourishing: positive emotion, engagement (which includes everything from warmth to ecstasy), meaning, positive relationships, and accomplishment. Being kind and caring is both a cause and an effect of this level of life satisfaction. I may not be sweet and agreeable all the time: I am beset by the usual human complement of not-so-nice emotions—anger, envy, worry, and selfishness, to name a few. But I work hard at not expressing them inappropriately and even harder at transforming them. Just putting a mask on what the Buddhists call "afflictive" emotions isn't sufficient. Invariably, how we really feel will leak out, with consequences for those around us as well as for ourselves. In *Social Intelligence*, Dan Goleman describes research at Stanford University on the effects of suppressing emotion. For the study, two women watched a documentary about the aftermath of the atomic bombing of Japan in World War II, and then discussed how they felt. One woman openly expressed her distress. The other woman seemed indifferent. (Unbeknownst to the first woman, the second had been instructed to suppress her emotions.) You can probably guess the outcome: the woman who had been forthcoming sensed that the other woman was hiding her real feelings and felt uncomfortable around her—in fact, said she wouldn't want her as a friend. But there was even more to it. The woman who suppressed her emotions also felt uncomfortable: she was tense and distracted, and in response to those stressful feelings, her blood pressure rose. The kicker is, so did the blood pressure of the woman who had been open about how she felt. "The tension was not just palpable but contagious," Goleman explains.

So how can we protect ourselves from the negativity around us, yet remain open and emotionally available to others? Empathy is at the heart of honest relating but it also leaves us vulnerable to other people's distressing emotions and moods. Part of being nice is maintaining our boundaries. We want to identify with others and resonate with their suffering, but at the same time not be overwhelmed with negative emotion, or merge so completely with the other person that we lose the ability to see the situation clearly enough to respond appropriately. Social intelligence, as Goleman outlines it, includes acting in our own best interests, as well as the interests of others. Empathy is a delicate balance: we walk a razor's edge.

When I'm angry or violent or sad, those around me are mirroring that anger or violence or sadness, often without even realizing it. And the converse is also true. That frisson of fear, that sharp intake of breath and "oops-a-daisy" sinking in your stomach you experience when you see someone slipping on ice is the same physical sensation you would have if you were the one about to take a tumble. Luckily, we don't have to actually fall to understand how the person feels.

This sort of mirroring goes on in our brains all day long as we interact with people. Our ceaseless mental chatter provides a running narrative of what's happening: it's the background music to our lives. Even with the volume off, others can still "hear" our song—pick up on our emotions, in other words. It's as if we are sitting on a bus listening to music through earphones, and the sound we think only we can hear is leaking out of the earphones and spilling over everyone around us.

But if moods are catching, the question is: don't we have some choice in the matter? After all, I'm a rational person, capable of figuring out what to do if, say, you suddenly throw a temper tantrum. I can think it through—that tantrum is *your* problem, not mine, so I'll just sit here and stay calm. Sounds good. But I only come to that conclusion *after* I've felt your temper tantrum coursing through my body. It's already my problem long before I'm conscious of what is happening and have worked out an appropriate response.

Nearly always, the first thing we notice about a person is the face. Facial expressions are a key part of our emotion-detection system, according to psychologist Paul Ekman. Ekman, who was the inspiration for the TV series *Lie to Me* as well as a program consultant, is a master at identifying microexpressions of emotion as they flit across the face, too quickly for all but a handful of people to identify. This rapid-transit system is how we communicate our internal states to one another, and the ability to read those signals is crucial for developing empathy as well as detecting warning signs. It would be convenient to say that nice people don't lie, but that in itself would be a falsehood. Our brains are exquisitely tuned to pick up lying, cheating, and prevarication—a survival tool we rely on to figure out who we can trust. Deception is part of being human, neuroscientist Michael Gazzaniga has pointed out: a world without it would be "awful," he says. (And a scary place, I might add.) Who would want to hear things like, "Gee, you look like you've put on weight," or "Sure hope your child grows into those ears," or "My husband thinks your sister is sexier than you"? The skill of crafting a well-calibrated white lie that won't cause harm is a mark of the socially adroit.

Even makeup and hair coloring are forms of deception, Gazzaniga says. But except, perhaps, in certain strict religious circles, I doubt anyone would consider it "not nice" to dab on a little lipstick and add a few blonde highlights. It might even be said that grooming is an aspect of being nice. Even people who aren't overly concerned with aesthetics appreciate it when someone makes an effort to look good. We prefer people who are attractive and tend to think they are nicer, kinder, and more intelligent than the less prepossessing.

It doesn't take a degree in neuroscience to have an intuitive understanding of human nature. Long before mirror neurons were discovered, or empathy became a household word, the nineteenth-century writer Edgar Allan Poe, in his short story "The Purloined Letter," summed up the process of reading the intentions of others:

> *When I wish to find out how good or wicked anyone is, or what his thoughts are at the moment, I fashion the expression of my face, as accurately as possible, in accordance with the expression of his, and then wait to see what thoughts or sentiments arise in my own mind or heart, as if to match or correspond with the expression.*

Just as we unconsciously mirror the facial expressions of a person we're taking to, we mirror the body posture and even the speech patterns as well, taking on the person's emotional state in the process. Here again, it's worth considering what we're passing on to others. A sullen clerk at the drugstore can start the day off on the wrong note, putting us in a bad mood that may take hours to unwind; meanwhile, we're infecting everyone around us. My personal Waterloo is the automated checkout machine at CVS, which never seems to work properly and barks out instructions in a loud recorded voice. Heaven help anyone who runs into me as I leave the store, before I've had a chance to get my anger under control.

As we look deeper into the social brain, it becomes clear why meditation is such a useful tool for managing emotions. Researchers in Richard Davidson's lab have been putting

Tibetan monks who are experienced meditators into functional magnetic resonance imaging (fMRI) scanners to see how these practices affect the brain and, hence, our moods. Loving-kindness meditation, which involves consciously directing compassionate thoughts to oneself and other people, lights up the parts of the brain thought to be the seat of empathy. Not only are we hardwired to care about one another, but compassion is a skill we can develop further.

Being kind and caring, then, isn't something we arbitrarily pull out of the air. Nor is it a posture toward others that can only be acquired through a laborious training process. To be sure, conscious attention and practice can hone these inbuilt skills. But unless we have deficits in the brain areas associated with prosocial thoughts and behavior, the instinct for compassion is always there, poised to respond to the appropriate stimulus on the right occasion.

Nice Survey participants related tale after tale of spontaneous acts of kindness they had received or observed. Some marveled at help that arrived from unlikely quarters, often strangers. Philip Ryan, a web editor, recalled an incident that took place near his office in downtown Manhattan:

> *A fruit delivery man, who was probably less than five feet tall, was struggling to push his overloaded hand truck over the curb. The boxes were stacked high, the top few rocking from*

side to side, and just as he managed to maneuver the hand
truck onto the curb, the stack toppled and boxes flew every-
where. One box burst open—luckily, it contained bananas in
plastic bags. Several people walked by, sidestepping the mess.
Then a little old lady who must have been at least eighty
stopped and, with obvious effort, bent over and started load-
ing bags of bananas back into the box. New Yorkers are often
viewed as cranky and self-interested, but this lady started
helping without a second thought.

From an evolutionary standpoint, caring for others—
especially kin—is a natural part of communal life. Empathy,
according to primatologist Frans de Waal, evolved for two
reasons: responding to the needs of our offspring and coop-
erating with our social group. "We do better if we are surrounded by healthy, capable group mates," de Waal explains.
"Taking care of them is just a matter of enlightened self-
interest."

Sometimes, however, we need to give ourselves a push. We
are pulled in so many directions in our busy lives these days
that, no matter how motivated we are, we can't answer every
cry for help. At times, we find ourselves torn between two
worthy concerns competing for our attention. There's a study
of helping behavior that was conducted at the Princeton
Theological Seminary, with students as the subjects. Some of
the students were assigned to read the parable of the Good

Samaritan and told that afterward, they should go across campus and deliver a sermon on the text. The researchers found that even the students who had just read the parable were no more likely than those who hadn't read it to stop and assist a man who was lying slumped in a doorway. The biggest factor in whether or not people would stop to help was how much of a hurry they were in to get to their next appointment.

I'm still haunted by my own behavior in a similar situation. I was scheduled to give a talk to a spiritual group, and while walking to the church I happened on a bizarre and upsetting scene: a taxi had flipped over in the middle of Park Avenue, a busy thoroughfare, and a couple of people were trying to right it. It was unclear exactly what had happened, but I had a terrible, queasy feeling that anyone who was still in the cab was almost certainly dead or injured badly. I asked a doorman watching from the sidewalk if anyone had summoned the police and an ambulance. His reply was noncommittal. I didn't have a cell phone with me, but I eventually persuaded him to go into his building and make the call. At that point I was torn. If I stuck around until help arrived I would be late for my speaking engagement, and I had no way to reach the organizers. But I also felt guilty about leaving the scene when no one else seemed concerned. Underlying all that was my dread of seeing any passengers who might be in the cab. Convincing myself that help was on the way and there was nothing more to do, I went on to my appointment. I still wonder, however, if there was something else I could have done.

As it happens, it's not uncommon for people to balk at helping, especially if it would mean interrupting a crime in progress or dealing with someone who is seriously injured. Sometimes we hesitate for a reason as basic as not being able to stand the sight of blood. Other times we may feel that the situation calls for more expertise than we can offer. And then, too, there is what is known as "the bystander effect." Research shows that when there is more than one bystander at the scene, the odds that any of them will help go down. That familiar "somebody else will take care of it" attitude takes over. Mercifully, however, there are people who reflexively overcome their inertia and, whenever they see a need, pitch in.

Psychology traditionally has ascribed self-serving motives to altruistic acts: we're only moved to help when there's something in it for us, even if that something is merely to relieve the guilt we'll feel if we don't lend a hand. No doubt about it, guilt is a powerful motivator. But once that initial step is taken, very often a genuinely selfless, compassionate instinct takes over. Medical personnel and emergency workers are, by training, programmed to help, and are protected from lawsuits by Good Samaritan laws. Even so, some are reluctant to step in at times. On airline flights, it's not uncommon to hear an urgent call for a doctor. Some physicians even carry

basic medications for just such occasions. One doctor, a gynecologist, recalled a time when he ignored the call for assistance, hoping a physician more qualified in emergency
medicine would answer it. An hour later, however, there was
a second SOS. This time he responded and found a toddler
shrieking in pain, the toes of one foot turning blue. A too-
tight plaster cast had cut off the circulation in her leg. He
quickly removed the cast, and the little girl's relief was immediate. Since then, the doctor always responds to in-flight calls
for help. "I never want that feeling again of a kid suffering like
that when I could have done something sooner," he says.

Most of the time, of course, our interactions with others
aren't premised on one of us being sick or injured or in trouble. Social connections permeate every area of our existence.
Nicholas Christakis and James Fowler, who have been
researching how social networks shape our lives, concluded
that we are connected not by six degrees of separation, as
Stanley Milgram determined in the 1960s, but by just three
degrees of separation. Even people we don't know, if they are
networked to us, can influence everything from how much
money we make to whether or not we lose weight to how
happy we are. "Social networks have value precisely because
they can help us achieve what we could not achieve on our
own," Christakis and Fowler explain.

Ever since the first settlers landed at Jamestown, Virginia,
Americans have been helping one another with everything

from barn-raising and quilting bees to investment clubs and twelve-step programs. Signal events in particular seem to bring out the best in us, sending us into helping mode. Alexandra Kayolanides, a graduate student at Yale and one of our Nice Survey respondents, explained how her cousin's new baby prompted an unexpected offer of assistance that ended up bringing her family closer together:

> My cousin Shannan had twin boys, and obviously had her hands full. Her parents stayed with her for a few weeks to help with the first diaper changes and burpings and crying, but after they left she struggled to find the help she needed. Our uncle's wife, Lisa, relatively new to our family, found herself out of work, so she volunteered to spend a few weeks caring for the twins and Shannan. Reflecting on the time and energy Lisa selflessly offered my cousin and her family . . . I marvel at how nice she was through all this. It makes me joyous that the twins cultivated a bond between Lisa and our family.

Moving is another event high on the life-stressor chart that seems to elicit our natural inclination to help. Survey participant Nicole Shaver, an administrator at a physical therapy facility, described her fortuitous moving-day encounters:

> I had only a cabful of things left to move, so I figured I could do it on my own. I made a few trips down the stairs and was

waiting on the curb for a taxi. When I picked up a box of Christmas ornaments, the box broke, scattering the ornaments everywhere. I was trying to gather everything when the owner of the bodega I was standing in front of and a homeless man who always hung around in front of my building rushed over and helped me pick up everything and load it in the cab. When I got to my new apartment, the cab driver helped me unload everything in front of the building. It was a day of pleasant surprises that made me realize you find amazing people where you would never look.

The double whammy of a new baby *and* a move nearly did in my niece Meg Morse, another Nice Survey participant. Then help arrived, reminding her that life is a cooperative effort. Here's how she remembered that day:

Six weeks after the birth of our son, we moved into a new house. I was working part-time and trying to figure out how to survive these new challenges. We were living out of boxes and had only a couple of plates, glasses, and pots unpacked. Just when I was beginning to despair that I would never cook a real meal in my new kitchen, my friend Margi brought her fourteen-year-old son, Bridger, over on a Saturday morning. They spent most of the day unpacking every box in the kitchen. Margi insisted that I sit with my son and simply tell them where to put things. When most people speak of generosity, they refer to monetary gifts. But to me, Margi's and Bridger's willingness to give of their time to help an overwhelmed and exhausted new mother was without a doubt one of the most generous gestures I have ever experienced.

Gratitude is a gracious—and expansive—virtue. Like kindness, it often fosters "pay it forward" giving behavior. Gratitude makes people want "to share and increase the very good they have received," says psychologist Robert Emmons, who has studied the subject for years. "I've concluded that gratitude is one of the few attitudes that can measurably change people's lives." As Emmons sees it, gratitude is a posture of humility that acknowledges how much we owe other people for all we have—and are—today.

Social networks "tend to magnify whatever they are seeded with," Christakis and Fowler say. On the plus side, networks "influence the spread of joy, the search for sexual partners, the maintenance of health, the functioning of markets, and the struggle for democracy." (On the negative side, they can spread depression, obesity, violence, even suicide and financial panic.) Spreading positive emotions and healthy habits helps cement the network, according to Christakis and Fowler. Nice people specialize in this. Their basic enthusiasm for life and other people suggests that they are likely to be concerned with the well-being and cohesion of whatever group they're in.

* * *

Apart from family, friends are the most important links in our social network. Research shows that people with a wide social circle and close confidants are healthier and happier and live longer. To the ancient Greeks, friends were far more than a hedge against loneliness and ill health. "In our youth, they help us to correct our faults, in old age they wait upon us and perform those necessary tasks for which weakness has incapacitated us, and in the prime of life they stir us to noble deeds," Aristotle said.

Whether or not our friends stir us to noble deeds, they certainly inspire us in myriad ways, sometimes with actions that speak louder than words. Mark Rogosin was that sort of person, according to his friend Clark Strand, a writer and Buddhist meditation teacher who participated in the Nice Survey. As Strand explained, Rogosin touched many lives:

> *Mark Rogosin was a New York patent attorney who fell through a hole in mainstream American culture sometime around 1980 and moved to Woodstock, New York, where he spent the remainder of his life copying the Tibetan Buddhist mantra OM MANI PADME HUM ("Behold! The Jewel in the Lotus!") onto small stones and scraps of paper, which he would then hand out on the streets of Woodstock to anyone*

who would receive them. These simple gifts were invariably accompanied by a smile and a thumbs-up sign of friendship, but were rarely accompanied by words, since Mark preferred to express his good will through silence, the universal language of peace and love.

When Mark died, we decided to institute an annual holiday called "Mani Day" on his birthday, copying the mantra onto stones all day and handing them out on the village green as he had done. When I passed out a flyer for this event, those who heard he had died often wept right there on the street. Probably one in four people who had come to live in Woodstock at some point over the past thirty years told me that Mark had been the very first person to greet and welcome them when they moved to town.

These days we move so much, and so often live at a distance from our families, that the role the family has traditionally played in many cases now falls to our friends. We celebrate each other's triumphs: landing a job, winning a prize, getting married, bearing a child. We commiserate over the tragedies: losing a job, getting a divorce, failing to make the team. We console one another in times of sickness or injury or loss. And we confide in each other endlessly, confessing our foibles and fears and deepest wishes, swearing not to tell another soul.

At their best, friendships are the most egalitarian of relationships—models of give-and-take. I phone you in a

dither over some real (or imagined) crisis; you drop everything and hear me out, then read between the lines and grasp
what's really bothering me, offering feedback and, perhaps,
wise advice. Another day, I do the same for you. We exchange
books, recipes, and expertise. We discuss politics, religion,
and every other subject that's taboo in most social settings.
Best friends lean on each other in equal measure, taking turns
being the focus or the cheerleader, the strong one or the one
in need. We may be as alike as identical twins who finish each
other's sentences—or so different that we marvel we ever got
together and revel in the fresh perspective our improbable
friendship brings. Either way, we're loyal. When something
goes wrong, we expect a good friend to take our side—or at
least have the grace not to take the *other* side. A gifted friend
is part diplomat, part therapist, part holy fool, knowing when
to speak up, when to listen, and when to make us laugh at
the sheer absurdity of life.

We asked the Nice Survey participants to describe someone they consider especially nice. A number of them singled
out a friend. Barbara Grande, a psychotherapist, mentioned
her "dear friend Suzie, who is always available with a sense
of humor." Another therapist, Sandra Weinberg, also cited a
friend named Suzi, saying she "is always wholeheartedly present, generous with her time, caring, and unpretentious.
Although she has a very significant CV, she is natural and
down to earth. Her wisdom is held in compassion."

A good friend can be a playmate and partner in crime. We laugh together, swap gossip and silly stories, and dare each other to do things we would never do on our own. My friend Mary and I are Lucy Ricardo and Ethel Mertz, getting ourselves into all sorts of scrapes that may not be funny in the retelling—just ask her husband—but were hilarious to us at the time. Good friends bring out the best in each other.

Men tend to form "buddy" friendships, getting together to play sports or watch them, or to paint someone's garage, or to shoot the breeze about women, work, and politics over a couple of beers. What men generally don't want from their friends is unsolicited advice. Not that they don't appreciate a friend who shows genuine interest. Scott Russell, who answered the Nice Survey, mentioned his friend Robert: "He is the only person I know who is totally grounded and always seems concerned about other people. He will always ask about my other half, and want to know how I'm doing."

Some men don't have male friends, and will venture into emotional waters only with a spouse or partner or woman friend. Women, on the other hand, tend to communicate openly and often. If you've ever eavesdropped on two good friends, you'll probably hear the conversation veer between relationships, current events, office gossip, clothes, family, diets, health, what they're reading, last night's *Housewives of ...* episode—and back again. Some of the warmest friendships for many women are long-standing ones among members of a group. Several evenings a week, Eleanor Wiley, a prayer bead designer and an author, meets up with friends for a walk around their neighborhood in Alameda, California. Their steady pace is punctuated by conversation on every conceivable topic that touches their lives. The women call themselves the Walkie-Talkies, and they've been walking together for more than a decade, although they've been friends for over forty years. There's a sixteen-year spread in their ages, but that's irrelevant when it comes to offering mutual support. Across the country, in New York City, a group of women writers who call themselves the Witches walk around the Central Park reservoir two mornings a week; by all accounts their conversation is as far-reaching as the Walkie-Talkies'. Several times a year, the Witches meet for dinner in a fancy restaurant.

Gift-exchange is one of the perks of friendship. A good friend will surprise you with a small treasure you never knew existed or wouldn't in a million years buy for yourself. A columnist for *Town & Country* lamented that the exchange of special, thoughtful presents among friends has given way to "receiving" a charitable donation made by someone else in your name. One Christmas someone gave me a pig—or was it part of a pig?—that ostensibly was going to a family in rural South America. Much as I applaud charitable giving and ache to help families in need, that had been a bleak year and was looking to be a bleaker Christmas. I almost would have preferred taking delivery on the pig.

But gifts between friends don't have to be material to be well received. One year I was writing a magazine article about gifts that involve more love than money and decided to field-test some of the ideas. One suggestion was to give someone a day of your time. With trepidation, I offered the gift to a photographer friend. Happily, it turned out that time was something she desperately needed—in her case, to help sort through and file hundreds of negatives. (Yes, this was the pre-digital era.) We spent one of the nicest days of our friendship sipping tea, talking, and organizing her negatives while her large Persian cat padded back and forth between us. As she reminisced about the stories behind some of the photos, I learned more about her than I had in a dozen conversations over coffee or lunch.

One of the most meaningful gifts a friend can give us is unconditional acceptance. Heidi G., a high school English teacher who participated in the Nice Survey, described her best friend as "an exemplary person" who is "kind, loving, thoughtful, loyal, considerate, and completely accepting of me for thirty years."

Sometimes friendship means rushing a friend to the emergency room, or bringing her home from the hospital after surgery, or dashing around getting crushed ice and the nurse's attention when she's bedridden in the hospital. I've been on both ends of those ministrations and am immensely grateful to the friends who stepped in. Nursing duty is not something I require of a friend—some people can't bear anything to do with illness or injury; we love them for other reasons. But not running in the other direction when a friend is facing a challenge is truly a form of selfless giving.

One of the most striking examples of selfless service is what my sister's friend Georgeanne did for their mutual friend Carol. At the time, Carol was terminally ill. She had suffered a stroke years before and was confined to a wheelchair with an oxygen tank strapped to her back. But she desperately wanted to attend her daughter's commitment ceremony in California. Georgeanne volunteered to go with her. Boarding the plane at the Seattle airport was the first challenge. Carol had to be moved to an electric cart, then to a wheelchair, then loaded onto the plane where Georgeanne had arranged for a special seat. When they touched down in San Francisco, Georgeanne repeated the process in reverse. For the next four days she shuttled Carol in her wheelchair back and forth between motel room and banquet hall and a city park, then loaded her back onto the plane for the return flight home. On board, Carol suffered some sort of attack. But as my sister later reported, throughout the trip, Georgeanne never lost her composure, displaying grace and good humor during what for most people would have been an ordeal. Carol died five days after returning home, but through Georgeanne's generosity, she had been able to share in her daughter's joy. Afterward, Georgeanne had only one thing to say: *It was a wonderful experience—and she was glad she could help.*

Childhood friendships are especially poignant. Some start early and last forever. Others, no matter how strong, fade into memory. Occasionally, I think about a kindergarten class-mate I haven't seen or heard of in decades, who befriended me when no one else would. My family had just moved north from Kentucky, midway through the fall semester. I was a late arrival freighted with a heavy Southern drawl. All my classmates avoided me except Rufus. I can picture us on the playground, standing in the shelter of a small tree. Rufus's mother had died not long before, and I've always wondered if that gave him a sensitivity way beyond his five years. All this time later, I am still moved by his kindness.

The end of a friendship can be as wrenching as the end of a marriage or love affair. Some peter out—death by attrition; some end by mutual consent; some crash and burn. Experts suggest that rather than staging a scene and breaking up altogether, it is better to use indirection—"defriending" the person on Facebook, not returning his calls, telling her you're too busy to get together—at least until you're sure you will never, ever want to be friends again. One friendship I've had for many years cycles through phases, like the moon. Some-times we go for years without speaking, but without rancor. Then something brings us together, and we resume as if no time had elapsed until after a while the friendship goes dark again. It seems to work for us, but it would have been unfathomable to my sister, whose greatest gift was cultivating her friendships, some going back to grade school.

Not everyone has a wide circle of friends. In fact, the average number of confidants has dropped from four to two. No one can possibly maintain more than a handful of close friendships, but some people don't even have one. To invest all our love in a spouse or lover or parent is risky, however, and for most people, having no friends would be a terrible lack. Nice people form warm friendships and make the time and effort to nurture them. Getting to know people from other cultures and different socio-economic backgrounds makes us more open-minded and open-hearted. It's a cliché to say, "All __(fill in the race)__ look alike," but unfortunately research confirms that we have more difficulty distinguishing individuals from races other than our own. Continued exposure, however, dramatically increases our ability to see past stereotypes. People with good memories for faces are at an advantage. They seem warmer, kinder, and more respectful. Anyone who can put names to those faces will be perceived as nicer still.

The ability to attend closely to others is a salient characteristic of nice people. Part of that is skill at making them feel truly seen and heard. Oprah Winfrey, in the last broadcast of her TV show, reviewed lessons she had learned in a quarter of a century on the air. "I found that everybody wants the same thing—validation," she said. There is nothing more irritating than being with someone whose attention is divided—the cocktail party syndrome. Instead of fixing his gaze on you, the person you're talking with is looking over your shoulder and scanning the room. Regardless of what he's really thinking, we feel as if he's casting about for someone more interesting to talk to. And sometimes, in fact, he is. Being nice does not mean we have to martyr ourselves to the party bore and listen to her drone on endlessly about . . . well, whatever. What truly nice people do in such situations, however, is draw on the many strategies that exist for politely exiting a conversation. And sometimes, in the process of, say, trying to see life through the other person's eyes, we suddenly find to our surprise that the bore has miraculously transformed. Nearly everyone has some aspect or quality or story to tell that is interesting or unique or distinguishing, but requires a sympathetic ear to draw out. It can be a personal triumph of sorts to discover the vein of gold in someone everybody else avoids. In the process, you can make that person's day.

Doctors are often accused of being brusque or distant, even rude, toward patients. Some of that, of course, can be chalked up to the punishing schedules they have to keep to, thanks to medical insurance carriers and managed care. But, even under pressure, there are limits. A friend who is undergoing follow-up treatment for lung cancer expressed relief that her oncologist was moving out of town. "He's really an awful man," she explained. Once when she complained about the discomfort she was experiencing from chemotherapy, he snapped, "Well, you could be dead, you know." It's always heartening to meet professionals in any field who have people skills. My dentist spends much of his day inflicting pain of some sort on his patients, but he is such a personable man and such an interesting conversationalist—not to mention blessed with the ability to understand sentences spoken through a mouthful of cotton packing—that despite all the drilling and scaling, an hour in his office is sheer delight.

One conclusion we can draw from all this is that our social world is where the action is—and our social brain is all-important as the activities director. Empathy is the key to relating to others. But despite what we know now about how our brains facilitate our interactions, not all the news is good. In a study at the University of Michigan, researchers found that in the thirty years between 1979 and 2009, empathy among students dropped 40 percent, with the greatest decline occurring over the past decade. Students' empathy was measured by how much they agreed with statements like "I often have tender, concerned feelings for people less fortunate than me." It is worrying if young people, the hope of the future, are losing the ability to identify with others. As we will see in the chapter on social media, too much time on Facebook and

Our social brain is all-important as
the activities director.

Twitter can fry the social brain. Online relationships lack the mirroring that is central to deep connection.

Perhaps all is not lost, however—empathy may just be rusty from temporary disuse. The neural equipment for it is still there. Two hundred fifty years ago, the philosopher Adam Smith spoke to our instinct to care for one another in describing the workings of empathy—or sympathy, as it was known in his day:

> *By the imagination we place ourselves in his situation, we conceive ourselves enduring all the same torments, we enter as it were into his body, and become in some measure the same person with him, and thence form some idea of his sensations, and even feel something which, though weaker in degree, is not altogether unlike them. His agonies, when they are thus brought home to ourselves, when we have thus adopted and made them our own, begin at last to affect us, and we then tremble and shudder at the thought of what he feels. For just as to be in pain or distress of any kind excites the most excessive sorrow, so to conceive or to imagine we are in it, excites some degree of the same emotion. . . .*

   Empathy—knowing and feeling what others are feeling
and being moved to help—may be the hot topic in psychology and social neuroscience today, and even, as we'll see in
chapter 6, in the workplace. But it's not as if we've just discovered how closely we're linked to one another. As Adam
Smith observed, however self-interested we may be, the welfare of others concerns us as well. And it's not just their suffering that moves us. Their happiness, too, is of prime
importance to us, even if there's nothing in it for us but the
pleasure of seeing their joy.

Chapter Four

································ ● ································

Why Manners Matter

anners may not matter to a hermit in a cave but they're indispensable when other people are around. Courtesy isn't time-consuming or complicated, like making a soufflé or learning to drive. And it doesn't call for grand gestures: consideration for others begins small. There's something refreshing about knowing that there are only four key phrases to remember: *Please. Thank you. Excuse me. I'm sorry.* Seven magic words that can take us far.

Of course, that's oversimplifying the matter. Not least because there are so many aspects of behavior to consider— and by no means universal agreement on their relative importance. On the face of it, etiquette is one thing, manners are another. The word *manners* comes from *manus*, Latin for hand. If etiquette refers to the rules of socially accepted behavior, manners relate to how we handle the rules and the situations they apply to. There's an expression circulating on the Internet that suggests the distinction between the two: "Etiquette tells you which fork to use. Manners tell you what to do when your neighbor doesn't"—doesn't know which fork to use, that is. Etiquette addresses the letter of the law, manners the spirit behind it. Good manners may even tell you to flout the rules in order to put others at ease.

Consider what happened at a formal dinner given by Queen Victoria. When the finger bowls were placed on the table before the dessert course, the honored guest, a foreign dignitary unfamiliar with the custom, promptly picked up his finger bowl and drank the water. To everyone's astonishment, the Queen immediately followed suit. Soon, the other five hundred or so guests were sipping from their finger bowls, too.

The story may be apocryphal but it makes a point: like Victoria, the well-mannered person would sooner commit a breach of etiquette than cause embarrassment or discomfort. Etiquette is full of opportunities to be embarrassed—land mines set to explode on the unschooled and unaware. Not surprisingly, it was Louis XIV of France—grandmaster of excessive gestures—who gave us the word *etiquette*, although happily we didn't inherit the extreme posturing and elaborate code of conduct that went with it. Etiquette, you may recall, is Old French for "ticket," referring to little cards posted around the grounds of Versailles or handed out to courtiers, detailing the behavior expected of them.

For the French aristocracy of the eighteenth century, proper comportment was the ticket of admission to the upper reaches of society. Nowadays, etiquette is often dismissed as mere window dressing: pleasant but hardly necessary—certainly not worth including in a discussion on being nice.

But if not here, where? And if not now, when? Maybe etiquette needs redefining. "The work of etiquette is to socialize the self," suggests Hazel Barnes, distinguished professor emerita of philosophy at the University of Colorado. "It reveals the values, beliefs, and presuppositions of the particular society from which it springs."

Barnes isn't talking about which fork to use, but something larger: what many people think of as manners. As we saw in chapter 1, for most of the past few thousand years, how we conduct ourselves has been considered a sign of character. Back in the seventeenth century, Edmund Burke, an English statesman, went so far as to call manners more important than laws. "Manners are what vex or soothe, corrupt or purify, exalt or debase, barbarize or refine us, by a constant, steady, uniform, insensible operation, like that of the air we breathe," he declared. "According to their quality, they aid morals, they supply them, or they totally destroy them."

Even Miss Manners—aka Judith Martin, whose droll wit

and spot-on advice have made her the etiquette maven for our times—takes a similar view. Obeying the rules of etiquette, she says, "is the oldest social virtue, and an indispensable partner of morality." Among the first things we're taught as kids is right and wrong behavior, she points out, and etiquette informs everything we do from then on.

Manners are a kind of diplomacy, a way of navigating through the endless loops and loopholes of our polyform, multicultural modern life. These days, we live in a United Nations of social expectations, and being nice requires an ear for the argot of whatever group we find ourselves in. What's appropriate on Park Avenue may be grounds for arrest in Harlem and vice versa. The nuances of being nice are not always obvious, obliging a well-mannered person to act like an envoy to a foreign country, recognizing that familiarity with the local customs is as important as representing one's own position. Even the simplest interchange can go wrong if we don't attune ourselves to the people and circumstances around us. Skimming the "Gestures" section of a few country profiles at CultureGrams.com selected at random, we can glean the following information: In Bulgaria, shaking your head from side to side means "yes," and nodding up and down means "no"— the exact opposite of how it's done in the U.S. Meanwhile, the thumbs-up sign, which telegraphs "right on" in France and America, is the height of rudeness in Albania, indicating "you'll get nothing from me." Mixing up a few gestures might not start a war, but it could derail negotiations or, at the very least, lead to miscommunication and hurt feelings.

Sometimes, of course, discourtesy is deliberate—done in jest, as in Aristophanes' plays, or Chelsea Handler's stand-up routines, or "dissing," the disrespectful put-downs endemic to the hip-hop culture. Generally, however, discourtesy isn't deliberate, but rather the fallout from a lack of awareness. Nice people may not be fluent in the language of the group—may not know all the unwritten rules of behavior—but you can be sure they'll pay attention and learn, or do a little research before inserting themselves into the local scene. It's all part of a basic consideration for others that seems to come naturally to some people but in reality may be carefully learned. A woman I know who is widely admired for her gracious ways spent the first eighteen years of her life in a Midwestern farming community, later polishing her manners by studying more worldly colleagues. What's notable about her isn't just her finesse but the fact that her good manners seem to emanate from a deep wellspring of empathy. Nice people have, or develop, an exquisite sensitivity to others.

This doesn't mean that the "socially challenged," as Caroline Tiger calls them in her pocket-sized guide *How to Behave*, are doomed to be pushed off to the children's table—relegated to the sidelines of life. If you can read, you can be polite. There are how-to books targeting proper behavior in every conceivable situation, from weddings, bar mitzvahs, and entertain-

> *Most of our day-to-day interactions are*
> *superficial encounters—brief exchanges—as*
> *we negotiate the ordinary business of life.*

ing the in-laws to teenage sleepovers, business travel, and online chats. And every week, it seems, another etiquette site goes up on the Internet. Some offer a conventional take on manners, others a hipper view.

Much of the advice they offer skims the surface: how to dress for an occasion, answer a wedding invitation, or politely tell the chatty Cathy seated next to you on the plane that you're not in the mood to talk. But when it comes down to it, most of our day-to-day interactions *are* superficial encounters—brief exchanges with strangers, near-strangers, and acquaintances as we negotiate the ordinary business of life. Shelves in the etiquette sections of big-box bookstores are groaning under the weight of how-to guides, the majority of them on how to stage the perfect wedding. Nobody, it seems, wants to spoil the big day by seating exes too close together or hiring the wrong photographer. But "polish" isn't just something to slip on with a dinner jacket or evening dress. People who have it, wear it 24/7.

It's tempting to think it doesn't matter whether or not we're polite to the checkout clerk at the supermarket, for example. But a simple human exchange like greeting her by name (isn't that what those ID tags are for?) may turn around her mood, which would be a service to everyone behind you in the line as well. (Consider it a kind of emotional "pay it forward.") Being friendly and courteous in moments like that is an easy way to practice nice behavior.

Not that courtesy and consideration aren't found at times where they're least expected. Socially awkward people who can't even pull off a simple "Hi, how are you?" are, paradoxically, often at their best when the stakes are highest: a neighbor's child is ill; a friend's beloved dog has died; the coach's team blew the championship. Highly charged situations call up emotional responses, and a klutz with a big heart may spontaneously say or do just the right, nice thing.

The most conscientious person doesn't get it right every time, however. Which is one good reason, Miss Manners says, that etiquette is critical at times of grave importance. Even preternaturally nice people can't be expected to slide through funerals, catastrophic illness, and accidents without ever putting a foot wrong. Formalities help us rise to any occasion, supplying a higher authority when bumbling efforts won't do. Knowing the rules not only provides something to fall back on but gives us the confidence to step outside the lines when improvisation is required.

That said, the manners part of being nice is increasingly under fire these days. So many young parents are ill-equipped to pass on good manners to their children because their parents never taught them. If you don't have a family dinner hour, it's hard to model table manners. And if you routinely fumble introductions, your children won't think polite greetings matter. For every little prince who shakes your hand, looks you in the eye, and says, "Hello, Mrs. Jones," or "Nice to meet you," there are dozens more who mumble something unintelligible, or don't even bother to look up from their Game Boys. In the past decade or so there has been a proliferation of etiquette courses offered to business people, privately or by their companies, just so they'll know how to behave with clients and on the road. Even the august Massachusetts Institute of Technology has instituted "Charm School," a one-day, degree-granting program. Students can earn a B.Ch. (Bachelor of Charm) by mastering etiquette basics like flirting, tying a bow tie, job interviewing, waltzing, and elementary table manners. The popular program—going strong since 1993—offers more advanced degrees (a master's or doctorate) to those who delve into the subtleties of manners with courses like "Apologies and Forgiveness," "Attentive Listening 101," and "How to Tell Someone Something They'd Rather Not Hear." Lest you think the need for this sort of remedial work is restricted to college students, consider this small example: in a workshop for experienced business professionals looking to change careers, only one of the dozen or so participants could pull off a proper handshake to the instructor's satisfaction.

Ours is not the first generation to perceive a need for

coaching in right behavior. Just as the bourgeoisie in Renaissance Europe looked to courtesy books for tips on how to act like gentlemen, mobile—and upwardly mobile—Americans from the late nineteenth century on have sought advice on genteel behavior. As etiquette books redirected their focus from being good to being nice, what became all-important was how to look the part; character development was a matter best left to a minister, priest, or rabbi.

But it's dicey to try to slide by on appearances alone. Eventually you're bound to be caught out. Without some sort of ethical foundation—a sense of decency, at least—"tips for travelers" won't be enough to secure acceptance in unfamiliar parts. Not for long, at any rate. Protocol can seem pointless or stodgy: why, for example, should British subjects customarily bow to royalty, and the American president customarily bow to no one? But just as every country or culture has its own traditions, every group or subculture, whether it's lawyers, golfers, debutantes, or Trappist monks, has its own code of conduct, and we tend to like people who make an effort to fit in.

Learning the secret handshake isn't sufficient. Nice people look and listen—and refrain from passing judgment on the habits and mores of the locals, however bizarre they seem. Being courteous, interested, and fundamentally well-disposed to others provides a cushion in the event you commit any gaffes. Unless you're up against someone especially rigid or cruel, sincerity and good intentions will nearly always win out. As the late Emily Post, queen of American manners for much of the twentieth century and still a force through the Emily Post Institute, put it, "Manners are a sensitive awareness of the feelings of others. If you have that awareness, you have good manners, no matter what fork you use."

The question of whether we're nice by nature or nurture is still debated, although the consensus seems to be that it's some combination of both. Aristotle and Confucius saw us as diamonds in the rough that the pursuit of virtue could polish up. The Buddha viewed us as pure and loving at the core—it's only because we haven't realized it yet that we behave like boors. To Sigmund Freud, we are forever teetering on the precipice of our unruly desires, saved only by the psyche's—and by extension, society's—rule-giver, the super ego.

Ralph Waldo Emerson called manners "factitious"—not natural but acquired—and said that in "persons of character," they arise spontaneously at the appropriate moment. A nice thought, and let's hope it's true. But without some sort of innate template for manners, some predisposition, could saturation in Emily Post really turn us into paragons of politesse?

Now we're back to the matter of whether the good and the nice are codependent. Certainly we all know people with impeccable manners who behave wretchedly behind closed doors and, conversely, people who are loving at home but pigs at the trough whenever they eat out. Would we call them nice? It depends. Even the nicest people have their moments, and we would be fools to hold others to a standard of perfection when we're struggling with our own behavior. On the other hand, if being nice simply meant being pleasing and agreeable, it would hardly be worth the bother. Rather than something we *do*, nice is something we *are*, even though we don't always show it. So assuming we all have the capacity to be nice, however broadly or narrowly we define it, how best do we go about it?

One way is to start young. As a small child I was given Munro Leaf's *Manners Can Be Fun*, a picture book with simple black-and-red drawings. First published in the 1930s and reprinted periodically ever since, it aims to introduce four-to-eight-year-olds to polite behavior. But with cheery directives like "Be kind to animals. They have feelings too," and "When I play with other girls we share our things and take turns doing what we like to most," it's clear that Leaf isn't simply doling out lessons in please and thank you, though he covers those as well. The whole argument that ethics and etiquette—the good and the nice—are confreres is summed up in the first two sentences of the book:

> *Having good manners is really just living with other people pleasantly. If you lived all by yourself out on a desert island, others would not care whether you had good manners or not.*

But *you* might. For the dirty little secret of manners is that they dog us everywhere. Once you know right from wrong in the etiquette department, breaching it seems like a violation of sorts. Think of that twinge of shame you feel as you take the last cookie, surreptitiously pick your nose, or gossip about a friend.

What's confusing today is that we seem to be getting ruder by the minute at the same time that we talk a lot about being polite. Bad manners are always something other people have—*and they really should do something about them*, we pronounce. It's a step in the right direction when we can take responsibility for our own contribution to the rudeness problem and make a commitment to be more considerate. Mitzi Taylor, a corporate trainer who self-published an etiquette guide, *Not So Common Courtesy*, posted the following goal on her website, notsocommoncourtesy.com: "I want to change the world one person at a time! I am passionate about people being respectful to each other and understanding that we are not alone on the planet."

The familiar phrase "common courtesy" affirms the idea that there's some sort of social compact around everyday behavior. Is something common to our culture only, or is it

We seem to be getting ruder by the minute at the same time that we talk a lot about being polite.

universally true? While the rules of etiquette are culturally derived, what we think of as good manners, or nice behavior, often has a broader reach. When behavior becomes widely endorsed over time, we label it common courtesy—and think well of those who live by it. Emerson again: "There are certain manners which are learned in our society of that force that if a person have them, he or she must be considered, and is everywhere welcome, though without beauty, or wealth, or genius."

It's debatable whether, in our plastic-surgery driven, appearance-obsessed, money-hungry culture, good manners alone would be sufficient to keep anyone at the forefront of society. But being nice undoubtedly gives you a leg up. And it doesn't require good genes, good hair, a trust fund, or a special wardrobe. It's democratic, demanding no particular talent beyond a show of kindness and consideration—ideally with a little humor and humility, and a dash of cheerfulness thrown in.

Like it or not, our behavior is under constant supervision. Unfortunately, we're more likely to notice misbehavior—and bad manners—than good. The Nice Survey asked participants to cite everyday behavior they found especially rude, and one of the main themes was inconsiderate cell phone use. Cell phones in elevators, on the bus, and in other confined spaces were a pet peeve to nearly all the survey respondents—and not just because it's irritating to hear a loud voice in your ear.

What's even more galling is being forced to listen to others' intimate conversations—or one side of them, at any rate. Priests in the confessional probably don't hear half the stuff that callers trumpet on the #101 bus. The only thing that's more of a turnoff, perhaps, is watching someone floss her teeth in public. Part of the problem is that, in recent years, the line between public and private has disappeared. It used to be rare to see someone performing a full hair-and-makeup job in public—unless she was stuck in traffic on the Ventura Freeway. But public space is now the communal living room, and many people no longer make a distinction between the two. At the movies recently a man and his pre-teenage son sitting behind us were unable to resist conversing through-out the film. Every time the boy didn't understand what was happening, he asked for an explanation, which his dad sup-plied at length. Despite requests to be quiet from everyone around them, they never shut up. We could only conclude that, to them, the theater was home—but with a bigger screen.

When efforts to quiet the talkers failed—they weren't even deterred by a plea from the usher—there was no choice but to put up and shut up, and ignore them. Even when right is on our side, we're reluctant to play manners police. Too often, the offender turns around and blames the accuser. In *Why Manners Matter*, Lucinda Holdforth cites a chilling case in which one moviegoer tapped another on the shoulder to ask her not to talk on her cell phone during the film, and the woman with the phone responded by calling the police and having the complainer arrested on harassment charges. The woman who complained was found guilty and fined! It makes those "What's it to you, bitch?" retorts seem almost refined.

Manners reflect the times, and few of us would want to turn back the clock. But as Emerson said, "Manners are very communicable; men catch them from each other." So the pressure is on to know the difference between good and bad behavior—and to choose the former. Granted, for all the talk about etiquette, there are few hard-and-fast rules—this isn't eighteenth-century France—and even the etiquette mavens don't always agree on what's proper. Courtesy is on a continuum, and often there are extenuating circumstances to consider. People who are attuned to their own and others' behavior are continually calibrating, if unconsciously, what is appropriate in the moment. If they're unsure, they can always ask themselves the money question: *What would happen if everybody did this?*—whatever *this* is.

That's one of the big questions the philosopher Immanuel Kant went on about. It goes to the point, common to both the good and the nice, that since we live in a world with other people, we have an obligation to consider their wishes and needs even if they don't conform to ours. The nicest people don't have a me-first approach to life. "Manners are used to establish a basis for other virtues," Miss Manners says. When you're not always trying to grab the first or biggest piece of cake, it's easier to offer the person next to you a slice. Most of the time there's enough to go around.

In one sense, it's very easy to be nice. It's a straightforward matter to learn how to eat politely or write a condolence note or invite the boss to dinner. When in doubt, there's that shelf of etiquette books to consult, or chat rooms offering peer advice. But the other face of etiquette is slipperier—the deeper meaning, where the nice and the good converge. This is where we need to summon empathy or generosity or compassion. A friend is gravely ill, or has lost a loved one or received a promotion; there's a wedding or a christening or a funeral we should attend; someone we know is going to jail. In matters of birth, death, triumph, and trouble, what is the nice, the decent thing to do? Are flowers in order, or a note? A phone call or a visit? Is it time to break out the champagne? Would a home-cooked dinner be what the frightened or discouraged or bereaved need to make it through the night? All these decisions come under the heading of manners, at least in the way Emerson described them: "What are they but thought entering the hands and feet, controlling the movements of the body, the speech and behavior?" Manners start in the head; intention impels our actions.

Miss Manners doesn't dwell on the how-to-treat-the-servants stuff that her pre–World War II predecessors covered at length; her concerns are ours. You have a perfect right to ban smoking in your house, she says, but "righteously hounding" smokers is decidedly bad form. Miss Manners is herself "unfailingly polite," she tells us, but she isn't a pushover. Thank heavens for that. Some of today's etiquette books call for Jesus-like forbearance. But people—even the nicest ones—aren't saints. If we can be arrested for asking someone to pipe down in the movies, what are we supposed to do with justifiable anger? Miss Manners proffers her own "meager arsenal," consisting of "the withering look, the insistent and repeated request, the cold voice, the report up the chain of command, and the tilted nose." When those ploys fail, she draws on "the ability to dismiss inferior behavior from her mind as coming from inferior people." It beats being arrested.

The prevailing view on manners, however, is that, insofar as possible, we should act with the comfort of others in mind. Isn't it drummed into us that making people feel good is the key to successful social and business relations? Leave it to Miss Manners, however, to turn conventional wisdom on its head: "If you are rude to your ex-husband's new wife at your daughter's wedding, you will make her feel smug. Comfortable. If you are charming and polite, you will make her feel uncomfortable. Which do you want to do?" Nobody ever said being nice was easy.

Under ordinary circumstances, however, we do well to err on the side of assuming that people are more likely to listen to and trust someone who puts them at ease. Aristotle said that we "like those with whom we do not feel frightened or uncomfortable—nobody can like a man of whom he feels frightened." An American psychiatrist who trained with Freud was particularly struck by the pioneering analyst's "charming" manners, which "immediately gave one a feeling of ease and security."

"Charming," on the other hand, is open to a wealth of interpretations: even the self-serving and psychopathic may exude enough charm to put others at ease. Therefore, we tend to place a high value on integrity, on people whose manners and morality seem to be of a piece—who live, not just speak, the truth. A conflict arises, therefore, when we're confronted with a situation in which it's very likely that the truth won't be nice. Does integrity always trump manners? Is it ever better or even best to lie? Once, I was traveling with a friend from Beirut to Jerusalem in a *service*—a public taxi—during Ramadan, the holiest month on the Islamic calendar, when Muslims fast till sundown. At lunchtime, my friend and I pulled out the picnic we had brought along and offered food to our taxi mates, as is the custom of the region. And they, as expected, turned it down. But at sundown, out came their picnic, and with the loveliest of smiles—and hands that hadn't seen soap and water in days—they offered us some dates. It's rule number one of traveling not to eat unwashed fruit, but we didn't want to insult the family by refusing their generosity. What to do? Miss Manners wasn't there to help. Finally, with slight of hand we managed to secret the dates in a large handkerchief while thanking the family profusely and maintaining the fiction we had relished the treat. The dates, of course, weren't really the issue. What was at stake was something more important—the kindness of strangers, the local rituals of courtesy, and the extreme insult, in that society, of refusing a gift. In a delicate situation, we had no choice but to put ourselves in the others' shoes and think how best to convey respect and not cause offense.

"All people everywhere want the same thing—to be happy," the Dalai Lama often says. We're drawn to people who make us feel acknowledged and appreciated. "It is our nature to enjoy giving and receiving compassionately," explains Marshall Rosenberg, creator of Nonviolent Communication, a method of facilitating interpersonal relations that is grounded in mutual understanding and respect. We're constantly having to reconcile what we want with what others want, so negotiating a solution that benefits everyone involved is a necessary, albeit challenging, aspect of being nice. But as obvious as that seems, how much more common it is to try and manipulate situations to our advantage.

One of the most exquisite forms of etiquette is *adab*. Sadly, it's a code of conduct Westerners seldom encounter or fully understand. Modeled on the exemplary behavior of the prophet Muhammad and refined by the Sufis—Muslim mystics—*adab* remains a guiding principle of traditional Islamic life. "*Adab* is courtesy, respect, appropriateness,"

Shaikh Kabir Helminski has explained. The contemporary mystic Andrew Harvey described *adab* poetically as "the concentrated essence, the perfume of all the virtues combined. It's their emanation in beautiful, courteous, refined conduct."

In an interview with Frederic Brussat posted on the website Spirituality & Practice, Harvey related a story about experiencing *adab* in India years ago. He was sitting on the steps of a temple with his head in his hands, clearly despondent. An old temple sweeper nearby kept smiling at him, but Harvey paid no attention. When he finally looked up, the sweeper had vanished. But, in his place, Harvey found a full breakfast and two cups of tea. It was a gift of great compassion that had probably cost the sweeper half a day's pay, Harvey said. But "that is the perfection of *adab*," he explained, "exactly the right gesture, done with tenderness and refinement of spirit, and then the refusal to even contemplate claiming any reward from it."

How different from the self-aggrandizing acts of courtesy and generosity we see all the time. Simple gestures like asking after someone's health or their family's well-being, listening to a friend's heartache, or, like the sweeper, responding instinctively to somebody's need in the moment are ways nice people practice *adab*, even if they've never heard of the concept. In Islam *adab* covers every aspect of interpersonal behavior, from keeping promises and not losing one's temper to answering the door and carrying on a conversation with a visitor. It's all meant to be an offering to Allah, arising out of what Harvey called "a nobility of character, a desire to put people at their ease, a desire to celebrate the divineness of people, and a desire to create a divine atmosphere between you and them."

While the Sufis have perfected the practice of courtesy as a spiritual act, the fundamentals of good manners—kindness, generosity, integrity, respect—exist in every culture in one form or another. The root meaning of the word *adab*—"to prepare a banquet, to invite to a meal"—harks back to ancient rituals of host and guest. In early Greece, entertaining guests was a window into character, a demonstration of moral fiber. Hospitality—*philoxenos*, literally "lover of strangers"—came under the aegis of Zeus, lord of the pantheon, suggesting the importance the Greeks attached to welcoming visitors and offering safe passage to travelers. The Latin root of hospitality, *hospes*, means "host," "guest," *and* "stranger." To the Romans, entertaining was a demonstration of mutual respect. Hospitality was also important to the early Jews and Christians: both the Old and New Testaments hold up kindness to strangers as a sacred duty.

Today, although entertaining is still a significant part of how we interact with others, the sacred side of manners is lost. We are much more involved in what the sociologist Erving Goffman famously called "impression management." Like Shakespeare and Freud and others before him, Goffman saw life as a stage and all of us as players, continually engaged in efforts to present ourselves favorably to the other actors in our personal dramas—all of it aimed at getting what we want. "Regardless of the particular objective which the individual has in mind and of his motive for having this objective, it will be in his interests to control the conduct of others, especially their responsive treatment of him," Goffman writes in *The Presentation of Self in Everyday Life*. If that sounds awfully cynical, consider how much of your time is spent in looking for ways to put your best self forward, even for the most noble and caring of ends.

In an ever-changing and bewildering world, the idea that there is a set of rules parsing the fine points of behavior is seductive. But the essence of courtesy goes beyond the guide-books, and it's here that being nice really comes alive. All the well-meaning advice in the world is for nothing if we don't have a grasp of our own motivations and a feel for the needs of others.

When we asked Sharon Salzberg, a Buddhist teacher known widely for her teachings on loving-kindness, what everyday discourtesy bothered her most, she replied, "Leaving someone out of a conversation." Ultimately good manners—and being nice—are about inclusion: allowing each person a voice, then having the grace to listen to what is said.

Chapter Five

.... ● ....

Love, Love Me Do

E very adult should be able to love and to work, Freud famously said. But if it came down to a choice between the two, the smart money would be on love. "We are born to love," anthropologist Helen Fisher explains. "Romantic love is a human drive, one of three basic brain systems that evolved millions of years ago. The *sex drive* motivates us to seek sex with a range of partners; *romantic love* predisposes us to focus our mating energy on just one individual at a time; and feelings of *deep attachment* inspire us to stay with a partner long enough to raise our children as a team."

Intimate relationships are not for the faint of heart, however. They are our greatest joy but also, at times, our greatest sorrow—the source of our most memorable moments and our nastiest battles. When it comes to love and loving, almost no one is indifferent. But the subject is so vast that deciding what's nice in relationships is a nearly impossible task. There is research galore on what evolutionary scientists call "mate selection"—and the rest of us think of as dating, mating, and getting it on. But when it comes to figuring out love as individuals, we are not so easily reduced to studies and statistics. There are commonalities, of course—we're all human, with the same physical equipment, the same genes for love and desire, and hormones for bonding. But every relationship, every marriage, every flirtation is different from every other, just as there are many different reasons why we love one person and not another.

We all have relationship horror stories: the perfect catch who overnight seemed to grow fangs; the oh-so-attentive lover—a keeper, your mother said—who suddenly pulled a runner. But on the other side are all the tales of happily ever after or, at least, happy enough. Regardless of how many tries it takes, we are eternal optimists about love, approaching each relationship with the hope and confidence that this is the one that will be fulfilling and enduring.

The frog who transformed into a prince isn't just the stuff of children's stories. For all the relationships that begin with instant attraction—that's almost 60 percent—there are nearly as many that start with "He seemed nice enough, but there wasn't really a spark," or "We couldn't stand each other at first, then somewhere along the way, all that changed." My first boyfriend during my teenage years kicked off our romance by throwing a rock at me that nearly broke my arm. No, that wasn't a foreshadowing of rougher times to come. But it was a kind of primitive version of what happens in *The Taming of the Shrew* and all those thirties screwball comedies in which the man and the woman fling insults at each other while the sexual tension builds, then fall into each other's arms. This isn't uncommon. Hate is this close to love and, under the right circumstances, it can turn on a dime. There are many paths to love, of course, and each of us in a lifetime is likely to walk more than one. Some are smooth and straight, others twisting, still others uphill and rocky. But every path offers us an opportunity to find—and become—the kind, caring, sexy, attentive, loyal, and, yes, nice lover of our dreams.

We are never too young to begin. A photograph in *The New York Times Magazine* last May shows two teenagers in evening dress getting ready for their junior prom. The young woman, Rose, is pinning a boutonniere on the lapel of Gabe—her "best guy friend," as she describes him. It's a repeat of the grooming ritual couples have engaged in for eons. The caption tells us what was going through Gabe's mind at that moment:

> *Rose was a great date. She's an extremely nice person, and we are really good friends. When the prom came up, I made these fliers that said, 'Rose Peterson, will you go to prom with me?'*

and had my friends throw them in her classroom, and I taped
them to lockers and stuff. Everybody has a funny, creative way
of asking someone to the prom.

Bravo! For all the talk about teens tormenting one another,
how nice to hear two young people speaking so warmly of
each other. And if thinking up "a funny, creative way" to ask
a date to the prom is the custom in Rose and Gabe's school,
well, hurray! Let's hope the practice goes viral. It shows a level
of caring—and creativity—that augurs well for the relationships of those young people in the future.

This vignette reminds me of another imaginative proposal
I heard about. The couple in question were schoolmates as
children. She couldn't stand him then: "He was that annoying kid in Spanish class who was always trying to be funny."
But by senior year in high school, they were on the bowling
team together, and her antipathy toward him had softened.
They dated that year, and then through college, while also
dating other people. After graduation, they moved to New
York together. Over the next six or so years, they filled their
lives with shared activities: they bowled, took salsa lessons,
Rollerbladed on the West Side Highway in matching skates,
and trolled the city for new and interesting places to eat. Typ-
ically, she was the one who organized their adventures, but
he was always an enthusiastic partner. Then, last year, on
their anniversary, he surprised her with a poem he had

written. It was the key to a treasure hunt, with each verse containing a clue to a different landmark on their journey together. One clue led to the bowling alley, another to the dance studio, another to the restaurant where they had shared their first meal in the city. On it went—all day in fact—as they revisited one place after another, recapturing memories. Finally, the last clue sent the couple back to their apartment, where she figured they would eat supper and watch TV. Instead, her boyfriend proposed. Ecstatic, she called her mother to share the news, but there was no answer. Same thing with her sisters. She barely had time to be disappointed before the doorbell rang. When she opened the door, there stood her whole family, alerted earlier by her fiancé.

What's surprising is that the man in question isn't known to be particularly romantic, but he certainly outdid himself that day. The sheer inventiveness of the project, and the effort that must have gone into its planning and execution, set the bar high for anyone planning a surprise for a spouse or lover. Challenging, yes, but unless your customary gift exchange runs to Caribbean islands and Cartier watches, your partner probably doesn't have extravagant expectations. When it comes to doing something memorable for someone we love, even the simplest gesture can make a huge impact if it's delivered from the heart.

England's Prince William went to great lengths to propose to Catherine Middleton in a rustic cabin on a mountainside in the African bush. He wanted it to be romantic, he said, and therefore chose a place that already held happy memories for them. For most of us, that level of romantic getaway is way out of reach. But every couple has a handful of places that are special to them: where they met, where they had their first date, where they spent their honeymoon—even the ballpark or museum or bookstore where they idled away Saturday afternoons. Couples are often asked what they do to keep the romance alive. Nearly all mention somewhere they go to spend time alone together, even if it's only a beach where they take moonlit walks. President and Mrs. Obama got a lot of flack from disgruntled taxpayers for flying to New York City for an unofficial "date night" of dinner and a Broadway play. But considering that relationships thrive on novelty, experts say, and date nights that involve doing something new can fuel a marriage, a little private time for the chief executive and first lady seems to me like a good use of Air Force One.

For all the ways we can disappoint one another in love, there are many more ways we bring delight. Couples who stay together—better yet, flourish together—make an effort to work through problems, resolve conflict, and keep romance alive. No surprises there. But they also make time for the small stuff we never hear about—gestures that may seem incidental but speak volumes about basic love and consideration. Tyler Syroko, a physical therapist who participated in the Nice Survey, mentioned something his wife had done that made him feel appreciated and supported. "I had had a very stressful week, and she and I had fought in the morning. But she knew I had had a bad day, so she made me my favorite dinner and cookies." One man I know keeps a small screwdriver handy just to tighten his wife's eyeglasses when they threaten to slide down her nose. My sister reads four newspapers every morning, and any number of magazines throughout the day, clipping articles that might interest her husband and leaving them in a folder next to his place at the breakfast table. Whenever he has a business event to attend, she prepares a sheet of background information on each guest. Corporate wives have traditionally served as the unpaid, unsung support team for their husbands, but many do way more than the minimum to make life run smoothly for their spouses.

But maybe I'm getting ahead of myself, discussing the fine print of courtship and married life. Let's back up and look at how nice people find one another in the first place. Where do they meet up, and what attracts them to one another?

In one respect, meeting prospective lovers hasn't changed that much. Proximity is still a major factor. It might be a coworker in the next office or cubicle, or a client; the gym rat on the next treadmill or the yogi on the next mat; a fellow volunteer at the food bank; a next door neighbor. The more we see of one another the closer we become. And the closer we are, the more I like you. The more I like you, the more you like me. Love blossoms. There was a time when the only "nice" way to meet was with a formal introduction by family or friends, but all that is in the past. Although clearly it's injudicious to pick up questionable people in questionable places and expect something good to come of it, beyond that, there is almost nowhere that people gather that isn't a suitable spawning ground for romance.

Most of the research on dating and mating says that similarity breeds attraction. Regardless of where we meet, we are most likely to fall for someone from the same socioeconomic background, with similar politics, values, education, and religious beliefs. If you just groaned, thinking, *Oh, no, not more of the same*, then you are probably one of the personality types in the "opposites attract" camp. Helen Fisher has just the mate for you.

Well, not literally. Fisher, a research anthropologist at Rutgers University who studies romantic love and attraction, probably knows as much about the subject as anyone today. Fisher came up with a personality typology that can help us understand our own love style and figure out what sort of person is likely to be a compatible partner. Her previous research had already identified the activities of neurotransmitters—brain chemicals—associated with personality traits that cluster in one of four types. There are the adventurous, "drink life to the fullest" Explorer, whose brain is flooded with the novelty-seeking chemical dopamine; the conscientious, community-minded solid-citizen, the Builder, whose brain is bathed in calming serotonin; the high-powered, analytic, testosterone-driven Director; and the intuitive, empathic, estrogen-saturated Negotiator. Now that sophisticated imaging technology lets us track the brain in action, it's tempting to leave it to neuroscience to manage our attractions. But none of us carries around a portable fMRI scanner, so no matter how much we know about what's going on in the brain, we still have to approach love and desire the old-fashioned way, ultimately choosing a partner in a face-to-face encounter.

Or maybe not—at least at first. A fifth of all relationships today start with an online dating site. Still, relying on Match .com or Chemistry.com or eHarmony to introduce us is one thing, and using text messaging and Facebook to set up dates another, but for true love to truly blossom, in-person meet-ups are essential. So much of how we respond to other people is instinctual, played out at an unconscious level. (Remember those mirror neurons from chapter 3?) Love at first sight—or, more accurately, attraction at first sight—isn't a fairy tale. It takes all of one-tenth of a second to form a first impression of someone, and as little as three minutes of talking to decide if we might have a future together. Then we may spend hours, days, or months marshalling reasons why he or she is—or is not—The One. But that initial hit is all-important.

Emotions flood the brain faster and with more intensity

than thoughts, which by comparison, poke along behind. Research shows that the initial judgments we make about a person's competence, likability, aggressiveness, attractiveness, and trustworthiness tend to hold up over time. First impressions are hard to override—especially if the person we're attracted to comes in a good-looking, sexy, and charismatic package.

Young women especially are often drawn to the so-called bad boy first. It isn't hard to see why. "Rule-breakers are exciting," one psychotherapist observed. "They get your adrenaline running." From an evolutionary standpoint, it makes perfect sense. Testosterone-powered, rebellious alpha males are catnip to women on the prowl, according to evolutionary psychologists who have studied women's preference for "cads" versus "dads." Billy Joel offered a simpler explanation in "Only the Good Die Young": "I'd rather laugh with the sinners / than cry with the saints / The sinners are much more fun." Think Mick Jagger, Sean Penn, Hugh Grant, 50 Cent. For men, the equivalent is a hot babe like Elizabeth Hurley, Scarlett Johansson, or Angelina Jolie. The whiff of danger they exude is titillating in the extreme.

Fun and sex make a heady cocktail, but eventually the rational part of the brain kicks in. What we come to value in a partner in the long run is more complex than washboard abs or pneumatic lips. Evolutionary psychologists tell us that, at this point, attraction switches to the best bet for building a family. Guys want to hook up with a naughty girl, but they'll buy homeowners' insurance with a nice one who'll keep the house neat and give them heirs. For women, the underlying driver is finding the best provider and most reliable husband and father.

If all that sounds a little 1950s, it may be because it's hard to reconcile with what we see happening around us. Today, young women in their teens and twenties aren't walking around in gingham aprons, ringing the dinner bell. Many of them are acting more like young men, hanging out with pals and looking for commitment-less hookups based on sexual attraction. Both sexes are postponing the search for Mr. or Ms. Marriage Material. The median age at first marriage is now twenty-six for women and twenty-eight for men—even later, age thirty, for men in Rhode Island, New York, New Jersey, and Massachusetts, and age thirty-two for men in Washington, DC. When the time comes to settle down, however, researchers say that men are just as likely as women to be looking for stability, warmth, and emotional support.

Now that women are becoming more financially independent, the need to marry up and marry well isn't quite so urgent—although that doesn't stop anyone from subscribing to the old saw that it's just as easy to love a rich man as a poor one. (Or a rich woman, for that matter.) One New York billionaire who already had four divorces behind him would be a bad marriage bet by most people's standards, but smart, successful women were queuing up at his door until he embarked on marriage number five. It's not just the money that's attractive but also what he represents: a confident, tough-minded, high achiever who has proven himself as a provider and father. As for setting our sights on a serial divorcé, that's another matter: it does, however, confirm the eternal optimism we have about love and marriage.

There is a sense of partnership and equality in marriages today—at least in theory. Young couples shopping for their first homes under the watchful camera of cable TV shows like *Property Virgins* often say that one of their main requirements is a top-of-the-line kitchen big enough to cook in together. And it's not just divorced and single dads who are devoting Saturdays or Sundays to activities with their children. The men who score high points on the niceness meter can be seen shepherding their kids to the zoo or the park or the movies so Mom can have some quiet time for herself. A woman who wants a husband who is willing to take an active role in raising their kids is unlikely to choose a guy who races motorcycles on the weekends. (There are exceptions, of course: "bad boys" like Mick Jagger and Keith Richards have raised nice children, and, to all appearances, Ozzy Osbourne, now that he's sober, is a pussycat at home.) Similarly, a man seeking a faithful wife and stable home life probably won't propose to the party girl who slept with his best friend the night before his wedding.

That said, there is sometimes no accounting for taste in love, as we can tell just by looking at the couples around us. She's a slob; he's a neatnik. He spends half the year on a plane; she seldom ventures out of town. He looks like a movie star— George Clooney but better looking—while she gives new meaning to the word *plain*. There is clearly something here that we're not seeing. And the ways of the heart are all the more confounding when we try to pin down exactly what is nice in intimate relationships. Once again, it all depends.

We've already seen that nice can mean different things to us in different situations and at different times. In picking someone to marry, cuddly qualities like kindness, warmth, and generosity seem to be important. But according to a study of men and women in thirty-seven different cultures, so also are intelligence, dependability, and good health. Would we say good health is "nice"? Probably not. But we can look at health as a sign of self-care and self-respect, qualities most of us associate with nice people.

Online dating sites are premised largely on the idea that the more alike we are the more likely we are to fall in love. Long before Match.com—or Facebook or the Internet even— there was Operation Match, the very first computer dating site. A primitive effort by today's standards, it was set up by two Harvard undergraduates on the university's mainframe for students at Ivy League and Seven Sisters colleges. At the time, few took it seriously. It was something to do on a lark, deemed respectable only because the students who signed up were just as likely to meet one another at a college mixer or through friends as to be introduced via computer printout. (The one married couple I know who met through Operation Match are, as far as I know, still together.)

Look how far we've come: today's dating sites have memberships in the many millions—and a seemingly inexhaustible pool of potential mates for members to choose from. But with so many choices, how do we find that one "nice" person who is right? Consider the most popular site, Match.com. Aside from the predictable questions about physical appearance and demographics, the "screening" essentially involves uncovering mutual interests. The eHarmony site, which prides itself on bringing soulmates together, puts the emphasis on shared values—a good predictor of compatibility, according to experts. If eHarmony's advertising has any truth to it, the method is working. The site regularly runs TV spots showcasing its success stories, and unless these couples are just smiling for the camera, they look pretty content, even blissful. But a question remains: can we be counted on to be totally honest in rating ourselves on how warm or generous or interested in others we are—on a scale of "not at all" to "somewhat" to "very much"? And who is going to say "not at all" when asked if they endorse statements like "I like to look at members of the opposite sex" and "My emotions are generally stable"? People routinely lie on online dating sites about everything from age and height to marital status—and probably even interests and talents. If "everybody does it," does that make lying OK—or is it nicer to be fully disclosing? In the "real" world, self-revelation is nuanced. We can get to know someone gradually over time, disclosing personal information as it seems relevant and appropriate.

For psychological compatibility, the site to visit is Chemistry .com, Match.com's sister site, which Helen Fisher helped set up. The matches are based on Fisher's typology. Her four types are not simply catchalls of interests or values, but dimensional—suggesting fully developed personalities, warts and all. The type that is probably the most overtly "nice" is the Negotiator, notable for intuition, empathy, imagination, altruism, and a tolerance for ambiguity, as well as something called "agreeableness." Fisher defines agreeableness as "a constellation of many traits" comprising "sympathetic, cooperative, compliant, considerate, charitable, forgiving, altruistic, trusting, and warm"—a list with certain similarities to the results of the Nice Survey. The brain chemical associated with the Negotiator is estrogen, and although Fisher's research found more women than men of this type, it should be noted that both sexes have estrogen in their systems, just as they both have testosterone. According to Fisher, estrogen activity is behind the "web thinking" of the Negotiator—it balances activity in both hemispheres of the brain, giving the Negotiator the ability to synthesize many different bits of information into the big picture.

Since Chemistry.com is a dating site, figuring out your own personality type is only the beginning. The site also lets you know who you would and wouldn't be compatible with and matches you up to dating prospects accordingly. Generally speaking, the Negotiator's best shot at compatibility is with her opposite number, the Director—the least touchy-feely or socially skilled of the types and therefore most in need of the Negotiator's emotional literacy and diplomatic skills. Meanwhile, the Director's forthrightness and focus appeal to the Negotiator who sometimes finds decision-making a challenge. Both value independence and respect each other's.

The fact that Fisher's system also includes the less-than-perfect aspects of each type lends verisimilitude to the process. For the Negotiator, that would include a tendency to be nosy and overly involved with people's lives—potential hazards for anyone with such an abiding interest in others. Nobody's perfect, and an important aspect of being nice is having the insight and self-awareness to know when and how our behavior, however well intended, could be burdensome or annoying to those around us. Relationships are a hothouse for all our habits, best and worst.

To say that the Negotiator is the most overtly nice of Fisher's four types is really, however, to miss the whole point of this book. All along the thrust has been to show how *nice* encompasses so much more than "pleasant and agreeable." Fisher's other three types also have a number of traits that might legitimately be classified as nice—including some that a number of people might find even "nicer" than the Negotiator's assets. Consider creative, curious, optimistic, and generous—characteristics of the Explorer—or the Builder's patience and conscientiousness, or the resourcefulness and heroic altruism of the Director. In fact, exploring the dimensions of Fisher's types is a reminder of how broad the definition of *nice* can be—as well as how individual we are in what we find attractive. What I bring to the table when I fall in love may be delightful to my partner but nothing like what you're looking for in a mate.

If an online dating site is doing its job, we come away with at least a handful of potentially compatible mates to be road-tested in the "real"—that is, offline—world. We still need to seal the deal face to face; this isn't the land of arranged marriages or mail-order brides, after all. But our increasing reliance on, and the social acceptance of, online introductions are facts of twenty-first century life. In a large city, it's possible to live on the same block for decades and never meet your neighbors. Dating sites have brought the world to our living rooms, expanding the pool of eligible partners exponentially in the process. One of the men Match.com proposed for me is an emergency room doctor whose face I recognized immediately from his picture: I've seen him around my neighborhood. Very likely he works at one of the hospitals down the street.

But what are we looking for when we download those profiles or instant-message a likely prospect? Is it love and commitment we're after, or just a few drinks, some laughs, and sex? If it's just a hook-up or "friends with benefits," then if we happen to ask ourselves, *Is he [or she] nice?*, the answers are likely to be superficial: *She's pretty. He's hot. She laughs at my jokes. He has a sexy voice. He likes Thai food and jazz. I love her perfume.* Not much to build a future on. But once we decide that someone is worth pursuing more seriously, *Is he [or she] nice?* becomes a crucial question. Sexual attraction, so lusty and urgent in the beginning, can quickly propel us into stage two, the romantic phase. Then what? As Helen Fisher explains, "The chemistry of romantic love can trigger the chemistry of sexual desire and the fuel of sexual desire can trigger the fuel of romance. This is why," she warns, "it is dangerous to copulate with someone with whom you don't wish to become involved. Although you intend to have casual sex, you might just fall in love."

After romance, then comes attachment, Fisher tells us. The hormones associated with bonding course through my partner's system and mine. Vasopressin, secreted during intercourse, accounts for the male mating and parenting instinct. Oxytocin is the female equivalent. Released during childbirth, fostering mother-infant bonding, it is also thought to be a factor in adult emotional bonding as well. Touted as the "love hormone," oxytocin has been shown to facilitate interpersonal behavior in a variety of situations, including increasing trust and promoting generosity during research requiring strangers to split a sum of money while under the influence of the chemical. It has also been suggested that oxytocin may play a role in building stronger relationships by modulating the anxiety associated with romantic love. But before anyone rushes online to order a supply, bear in mind that more recent research has found that, yes, oxytocin increases warm feelings—but only toward those in your family or immediate circle, people with whom you have already bonded.

"Love is all you need," the Beatles sang, and as a life principle, that's probably right. But is it enough to keep a long-term relationship going? Conventional wisdom says that passion dies. So what helps us create a partnership that will endure? Ask any couple who have been together awhile what keeps them together, aside from sex, and they're likely to mumble things like loyalty, friendship, common interests, companionship, and children. But Arthur Aron, a psychologist who has long studied interpersonal relationships—and collaborated with Helen Fisher on research for her book *Why We Love*—suggests that the secret to long-time commitment is "self-expansion." In other words, how much do the partners broaden and enhance each other's lives? Do they introduce each other to new experiences? Do they contribute to each other's personal growth? Togetherness per se isn't going to

do it. Sharing routine activities like cleaning house or wash-
ing the dog or attending the children's soccer games won't
provide the kind of lift Aron is talking about. What he and
his team found is that "novel and arousing activities" are what
increase and sustain relationship satisfaction. Take your pick
what will be "novel and arousing" for you and your spouse or
partner. One couple I know take a long-distance bicycle trip
nearly every year through a different part of the world. They've
had any number of adventures on nearly every continent, riding through the Alps, California wine country, the French
countryside, and so on. No two trips are ever the same. In the
months leading up the trip, they train by biking a hundred
or more miles a weekend over challenging terrain. Another
friend introduced her then-boyfriend to meditation and yoga,
and they traveled all over attending retreats and teachings
by Buddhist masters. The young couple at the beginning of
the chapter—now married—have already started their relationship off on a path to longevity with their enthusiastic
embrace of new, shared adventures. Each couple have to
define "novel and arousing" for themselves. For some, it might
be building a boat together, starting a side business, racing
gliders, or taking a volunteer vacation to rebuild houses in
Haiti. Others might have a more sedate idea of "novel and
arousing." In any case, the idea is for the partners together to
push beyond their respective comfort zones. For a lab
experiment, Arthur Aron and his staff assigned couples to a

challenging physical activity involving gym mats and Velcro straps that it's safe to say none of them had tried before.

And then there are couples for whom the passion has never waned: even with years of marriage behind them, they insist they're as much in love as ever. What for them seems to keep love alive is not only pursuing new challenges but also keeping the communication channel open. Just as important, it seems, is what the partners *don't* do—namely fret about the state of their relationship. Questions like *Does he/she really love me?* and *Will it last?* are no longer burning issues.

While we may not be able to predict with certainty which relationships will endure, scientists studying commitment have found genetic markers of marital *in*stability: in a Swedish study, men who had a variation in what is facetiously called "the fidelity gene"—the gene that controls vasopressin—were less likely to get married in the first place, and if they did marry, were more likely to have marital problems. But genes are not destiny—we have choices—and we can train ourselves to resist temptation.

For years, women's magazines have been a leading source of relationship advice, and a few still are. Probably the most popular advice column among young women is "Ask E. Jean" in *Elle* and on Elle.com. "Auntie Eee," as E. Jean Carroll styles herself, is a former *Saturday Night Live* writer who wraps common sense in a little wit:

Q: *My husband works for a hedge fund. Since we got married six months ago, he hasn't touched me. He says he wants to get back in shape, but all he does is play World of Warcraft till 2 a.m. every night "to unwind." Help!*

A: A woman requires the same things from a hedge fund trader as she does from a husband—huge returns. Tell him that if your Night Elf does not soon receive an investment, he's gonna face humongous withdrawal fees.

Of course, the Internet contains a dizzying amount of relationship advice from peers as well as experts of all stripes. Read enough of the how-tos and you start to wonder, *Doesn't anyone know* anything *about love and sex anymore?* When we're in the throes of a relationship, however, we're awash in hormones and prior history, and we're not viewing what's going on with the objectivity of a therapist or an advice columnist or even our best friends. You may not be the type to air your problems in the media—most of us aren't—but if you pick through the welter of advice out there, there is actually some wisdom. Even the most self-aware person can always find something to learn in the realm of love and sex. Just reading other people's questions often gives us answers to our own. Listening to Dr. Laura obviously isn't the same as relationship counseling in the privacy of a therapist's office. But it should be reassuring to realize that media shrinks generally aren't shooting from the hip. To avoid massive law suits, they have to be extra careful of the advice they dispense. If anything, we're likely to feel that their advice is too generic to apply to our situations. But what we *can* conclude from all this free love advice is that whatever relationship issues we face, there are undoubtedly other couples out there struggling with the same thing.

Even positive psychologists, who are more interested in well-being than pathology, acknowledge that it makes sense that we're more likely to home in on what's wrong with our relationships than what's right. "Threatening circumstances" mobilize us faster than good times do, they point out, and relationship issues hit us where we are most vulnerable. When life is going smoothly, we don't dwell on it; we just live it. But when something disturbs that equilibrium—job loss, infidelity, death of a parent, a child in trouble, illness, loss of interest in sex, even just restlessness or mild dissatisfaction with one's partner or with the relationship itself—we look around for a solution that will make us feel better.

Relationship hiccups may start with something external but nearly always end up casting us back on ourselves. As one expert put it, the problem isn't your partner but how you're handling your feelings about your partner and whatever is going on between you. The nicest couple in the world can have issues with each other. The question is whether we can be honest with ourselves about the problems. How willing am I to assume responsibility for my part and communicate with my partner about finding a solution? Despite all the self-help books on marriage, relationship issues are not an easy fix. There are so many variables, and every couple has their own set of challenges. Tolstoy was probably right when he wrote, "Happy families are all alike; every unhappy family is unhappy in its own way." There isn't any one "nice" way to live harmoniously with another person, any more than there is just one way to be nice. But certain basics that seem to be helpful include self-honesty, a sense of humor, the ability to forgive, and, as a bottom line, kindness. In one study of the qualities people were seeking in a mate, both men and women put "kindness and understanding" at the top. Life is difficult. Most people want a marriage or relationship to be a safe haven, not a tug of war. A friend explained why she had finally split up with the man she had been living with for several tumultuous years. "I'm just too tired," she said. "I don't have the energy anymore to deal with the chaos he creates around him."

Not every relationship can be fixed, nor should it be. Abuse—physical or emotional—is the number one dealbreaker. But after that, what can test many relationships to the limit is a person like my friend's ex-lover: an emotional sinkhole whose all-consuming demands leave his partner gasping for air. While we're in the rapturous, madly-in-love period, our loved one's eccentricities (or outright madness) go right over our heads. But when the relationship moves into a period of consolidation—Fisher's period of attachment—personality traits that didn't bother us before may stand out in high relief. Histrionics, manipulation, and relentless bids for attention can quickly become too much to bear. Something has to give. There was an off-Broadway play with a title that aptly describes the tension of a relationship in this phase: *I Love You, You're Perfect, Now Change*.

What is *not* nice is to go into a relationship thinking, *He'll be great once I get my hands on him*, or *I hate that about her, but once we're married I'll make her do something about it*. Maybe that works with lowering the toilet seat or starting the dishwasher or squeezing the toothpaste from the end. But trying to change someone's fundamental personality is a fruitless exercise. People can change, of course, but only if they want to, not through coercion. As we might expect, couples in which each partner is genuinely accepting of the other are happier and more likely to stay together. I can think of one man I probably couldn't live with for a weekend, but his wife has been with him for more than twenty years and has every intention of staying. She's no pushover, either, She's well aware of his flaws, but there is much about him that she loves and admires. She accepts him, warts and all, and stands by her commitment, even on days she can't stand him. What could be nicer?

The Internet has made it impossible to claim we don't know how to do something—and that includes how to love. In addition to the welter of websites and blogs with advice ranging from the enlightened to the merely silly, we have those repositories of collective wisdom, Wikipedia and wikiHow. Under the no-nonsense heading "How to Love," wikiHow organizes its advice into six basic "Steps," twenty-some "Tips," and ten "Warnings"—with links to fourteen other pages on topics like "How to Tame a Free Spirit," "How to Have a Healthy Relationship," "How to Have a Great Marriage," and my favorite, "How to Explicate a Love Poem." (If your analytic skills are rusty, there are also instructions on *writing* a love poem.) Most of the advice is Love 101, consisting of basic truisms that, if you don't know them already, may explain why you have marriage troubles or difficulty handling any relationship longer than a one-night stand. Paraphrased, the six steps are:

Say "I love you" and say it like you mean it.
Be empathic: put yourself in your lover's shoes.
Love unconditionally, not for what your lover can
    do for you.
Give without expecting anything in return.
Don't cling, or idealize your lover.
Even if you've been hurt, don't give up on love.

Tempting as it is to sneer at the banality of these suggestions, the information clearly bears repeating. The fact that so often we overlook the basic principles of interpersonal consideration may be part of the reason the divorce rate in

America still hovers between 45 and 50 percent for first marriages, and rapidly escalates with each marriage thereafter. (Between 70 and 73 percent of third marriages break up.) Divorce lawyers say that 20 percent of the breakups in their caseloads these days are casualties of Facebook. In making it so easy to reconnect with old friends and lovers, not to mention carry on flirtations, Facebook has apparently made it easier to start an affair.

Infidelity is a tough problem to handle. As with other love problems, there's no one right way to deal with it, although some ways are probably nicer than others. Much of it depends on your intention. Do you want to stay and work it out, or is it time to go? A woman who had been married for a year wrote to Philip Galanes, the "Social Q's" columnist for *The New York Times*, wondering how to get past the fact that, on the night before their wedding, her fiancé picked up a woman in a bar and slept with her on a beach. It's easy for us to say, "Well, she never should have gone through with the wedding." But we also know why she did. Galanes gives the only advice possible: see a marriage counselor. Her query is a reminder that every relationship has speed bumps, but always the question is, *Is this one too high to clear?*

Researchers have found that rejection does more than hurt our feelings or our pride. Emotional rejection registers in the same part of the brain as physical pain, which is why getting dumped can feel as if you've been sucker punched. Arthur

Aron offers another analogy: when we bond as a couple, we start to feel at one with our partner, so if he or she leaves, it can seem as if a part of us is literally being torn away. All this is useful information to file away if it becomes necessary to end a relationship or marriage. No writing "We're through" in the subject field of an e-mail, as some people have, or sticking an "It's over" Post-it note on your about-to-be-ex's computer screen or the bathroom mirror; no leaving an "I'm moving out" message on your partner's voice mail. One woman—and I'm sure there are many more like her—found out her husband was divorcing her when he changed his marital status on his Facebook page.

What happens when the differences are irreconcilable? Even without slinging accusations, some marriages just can't be saved. In denial, we may cling long past the expiration date. Is there a nice way to leave? Something that's happening more frequently—largely because the economy makes divorce too costly for some couples—is the our-marriage-is-over-but-we're-still-living-together arrangement. What are the rules for *that*? How can we nicely cohabitate with an ex? Oddly enough, there are a few role models. Instead of silently fuming at opposite ends of the house, most experts recommend drawing up guidelines about cooking, chores, and, especially, finances; the goal is to keep resentment and bitterness to a minimum, particularly important when there are children in the house. Still odder, but probably nicer, is something else that's cropping up: couples who are amicably divorcing, then staying on in each other's lives, although not sharing a home. One couple even threw a divorce party, inviting all their friends. This wasn't a first marriage for either spouse, which may explain why dissolving it was easier. They were able to simply accept that their interests and lifestyles didn't mesh. But the message on the invitation they sent out could be an aspiration for other divorcing couples: "As we change the parameters of our relationship, our mutual admiration and caring is constant."

Whatever we do—or don't do—with or to an intimate partner, there's one thing that's almost guaranteed to forge a more caring and committed relationship: Be forgiving. Hurt and betrayal change the foundation of a relationship from love and cooperation to competition, notes Michael McCullough, a psychology professor at the University of Miami. The desire for revenge is inborn, he says, "but so also is the capacity for forgiveness." Loving relationships are too valuable, and the benefits too extensive, to risk it all by acting out fantasies of retribution. Forgiveness can help us shift the focus of the relationship back to love and cooperation.

But all that sounds a little lofty, perhaps. Where's the romance? After all, love, marriage, and relationships are matters of the heart. Many of the nicest love stories make their way into the "Vows" column in *The New York Times*. The marriages may not all be happily ever after; obviously it's too soon to tell. But the sentiments the couples express about each other—and others express about them—bespeak kindness and good will. One groom proposed to his bride with this simple thought: "I know you're perfectly capable of living this life on your own, but I want to live it with you."

I'd like to say that nice people are romantics. Or maybe it's the other way around. Someone once said that every birth signals hope in the future. The same could be said of every love affair or marriage. Walking through his neighborhood in Brooklyn, New York, Sam Mowe, a magazine editor who participated in the Nice Survey, saw the following message written in chalk on the sidewalk: "Dear Jade, Everything about you is beautiful and I'll love you forever."

············ ◆ ············

Chapter Six

When Kindness Goes
to Work

If love is one prong of life purpose, work is the other and, to many people, no less important. In fact, to some people—hedge fund billionaires spring to mind—work might even have the edge.

Work and the workplace are two separate issues, albeit in most cases, related ones. We may love our work but hate our workplace. Less often, it may be the other way around. Either way, it isn't easy being in the workplace today, wherever you are on the staffing chart. No industry or business or nonprofit seems to be safe from layoffs and cutbacks, mergers and downsizing. These pressures, plus the overall climate of economic uncertainty, are all contributing to feelings of unrest at work.

As managers forced to cut costs pare staff to a minimum

and strip the office of amenities of any sort, disgruntled workers, already in fear of losing their jobs and not finding others, are increasingly frustrated and disheartened. Many are putting in the hours but doing the minimum. Gossip and backbiting are rampant, as workers jockey for favor in an atmosphere that seems to reward competition over cooperation, and survival over basic kindness. When managers are bent on getting the most out of the fewest people, there is little staff enthusiasm and no sense of achievement for a job well done. So what's an upbeat, ambitious, capable, creative, and emotionally intelligent worker to do? It's hard to be nice in a den of thieves. A recent cartoon in *The New Yorker* pegged the dilemma. It shows a husband saying to his wife, "If you bring joy and enthusiasm to everything you do, people will think you're crazy."

Good news: not everyone will think you're crazy. There's an undercurrent in business that has been gaining momentum. Just as industries are slowly but surely introducing green practices, companies are giving more credence to the idea that being nice gets the job done. Caring, empathic, emotionally savvy people might actually be assets to an organization, not detrimental to the bottom line, as once believed. Two advertising executives wrote a little book in 2006 called *The Power of Nice*, with a subtitle that tells the story: *How to Conquer the Business World with Kindness*. A year earlier, the *Harvard Business Review* published an article, "Competent Jerks,

....

Companies are giving more credence to the idea that being nice gets the job done.

....

Lovable Fools, and the Formation of Social Networks," that gave form to an idea many executives knew intuitively, or at least suspected: namely, that most bosses will choose a like-able person with average competence over a highly competent person with lousy social skills.

So why do we keep maintaining that "nice guys finish last," and "it's dog eat dog out there"? When they're firing someone or making another tough decision, people love to repeat that line from *The Godfather*: "It's not personal, Sonny. It's strictly business." But the fact is, we're not plotting Mafia hits or even "killing the competition." All business is personal as long as people are doing the work.

Stress usually gets the blame for why bosses take out their frustrations on underlings or why coworkers sabotage one another but, according to some experts, that's not the whole story. Yes, there are unhappy, unproductive workers whose managers are abysmal at treating their employees with respect. But as the workplace becomes more diverse and companies do more business with companies and colleagues overseas, the pressure to be more people-savvy is increasing. No longer are warmth and friendliness qualities tolerated only behind the door marked Human Resources. A conservative office might shrink from using words like *kindness* and *empathy*, preferring terms like *respect* and *tolerance*, but when it comes down to it, the strengths of nice people—compassion, caring, generosity, and the like—have earned a place at the conference table. Increasingly, there's a realization that we can't possibly deliver a top performance if we're working in an environment that turns up the heat while failing to consider the consequences of so much pressure.

The ideal for any organization, of course, would be to find workers who are high in both competence and social skills. The *Harvard Business Review* article suggests that such people are in short supply, however. Those who do exist are often found . . . where? In the CEO's office. The hard-driving, take-no-prisoners, type-A personality is no longer the model for enlightened leadership. With so many frightened and disgruntled workers around, the boss with a heart is the one who can win the trust of his staff and encourage the best performance out of them. Nice Survey participant Don Harrell offered a good example of just such a leader from his days as press secretary to a governor:

> One cold morning when it was snowing hard, several members of the press were waiting on the porch outside the governor's mansion. It never occurred to us to ask them in. "Let 'em wait," we thought. But when the governor found out they were there, he said, "By all means, ask them in. Get some coffee for

them. Let them warm up before we start the press conference."
I felt like a dog, and so did the rest of the staff. He was right.
[Being nice] came easily to him, not as a politician (although
his political instincts were excellent), but as a human being
wanting people to be warm and inside, away from the snow-
storm.

That instinct for kindness seems to be especially well developed in some people, making them superstars of enlightened leadership who are role models for everyone else. By all accounts, Sheryl Sandberg, chief operating officer of Facebook, is just such a leader. Profiling her for *Vogue*, Kevin Conley singled out "her personal touch, her ability to reach out in a crisis, her tendency to promote people so they utilize talents they often do not even suspect they had . . ." But it was Sandberg's sister who summed up her gift: "She really sets an example for how people should treat each other."

Attributes of a successful leader now often include words like *decent, humble, authentic, appreciative*, and *kind*. Before he founded the workout sensation Zumba Fitness, Alberto Perlman had raised several million dollars to launch a business to seed Internet startups. When the tech bubble burst, Perlman had to fold the company. Instead of simply walking away, he decided to return his investors' money. "My father always taught me that if you're honest and respectful, it will come back to you tenfold," he said. Zumba's success is proof.

Executive-suite niceness invariably has a trickle-down effect. Companies that are considered nice places to work tend to have people-oriented values that are expressed consistently throughout the organization. Clothing manufacturer Eileen Fisher, a health-conscious yoga practitioner who has long supported self-development, gives all employees a two-thousand-dollar-a-year education and wellness grant to use for things like yoga, gym memberships, massages, and classes of any sort. The gesture not only "feels right," said the company's chief culture officer, but encouraging employees to develop new skills and grow as individuals makes good business sense.

PrintingForLess.com, an online printing services company headquartered in Montana, has a no-gossip policy that's not just talk: it's strictly enforced. Transgressors are given a good talking-to, and if the problem continues, they're fired. Good communication is one of the operating principles of the company. New hires are sorted according to communication style. Reds are direct—just give them the facts, fast. Blues want the details and time to absorb them. Spontaneous yellows seek a personal connection. Warm, compassionate greens value courtesy. Color-coded nameplates on the employees' desks indicate their communication styles, so coworkers know how to frame a conversation for the best results. Shayla McKnight, a tech service assistant at PrintingForLess.com, was skeptical at first that the no-gossip policy would work, but now she supports it wholeheartedly. It contributes to good teamwork, she said. And with no office grapevine, personal information circulates only on a need-to-know basis, at the discretion of the source.

Gossip is one of the most poisonous aspects of working today. With so much downsizing, speculation on who might be laid off floods interoffice e-mail and, once someone gets the ax, word sometimes gets around even before the fired employee has been informed. People with an open door and sympathetic ear often find themselves cast in the role of office mom, sob sister, and job counselor. Every organization has someone whose desk everyone seems to hover around, or whose office is somehow on everyone's way to wherever they're going, so there's a lot of "I'll just stick my nose in and say hi to him"—or her. Usually her. (Sorry, guys: when it comes to what psychologists call likability, there's a bias toward women.)

Likability is a big word in corporate America, as organizations wake up to the benefits of having personable people on staff. They're great networkers and skilled diplomats, good at getting people who don't normally work together—or don't work well together, or don't want to work together—to work together. And when people work together, they get to know and like one another, increasing the chances they will be more innovative and productive, and more likely to collaborate in the future. Just like that friend who is always the center of the liveliest conversation at a party, the office likability star can be a major contributor to the success of whatever project they're engaged in. Often the nicest person in an office is operating behind the scenes, supporting the rest of the team, like Amanda, the office manager at the magazine where Nice Survey respondent Alexandra Kaloyanides used to work: "She handled with generosity and without an attitude the dull parts of her job that made it easier for the rest of us to do ours."

Sadly, because skills like networking ability and good communication come naturally to women—they're wired into the female brain—traits like warmth and kindness still may not be valued as highly as those like competence and intelligence that are often associated with men. What's interesting, however, is to look at many of the women currently serving in the U.S. Senate: they are far more collegial than their male counterparts, routinely working across the aisle to get legislation passed. But in many companies—not just conservative ones—women feel the need to subvert the skills that come naturally to them in order not to be seen as soft or ineffectual by male colleagues. It's ironic, considering that one of the senators most known for his warmth, and networking and communication skills, was also one of the most powerful—Ted Kennedy.

To be effective in the workplace, being nice can't be faked. "Nice must be automatic," Linda Kaplan Thaler and Robin

Koval emphasize in *The Power of Nice*. But if your people skills aren't up to par, are you doomed? Luckily not. Empathy, experts say, can be learned or improved. Some companies are only too willing to offer coaching, figuring it will be good for employee morale as well as for the bottom line.

Working together breeds togetherness, and fast friendships in the office are common. Some are the kind of casual relationships marked by a little banter, a little grousing about the boss or the workload, and maybe some chat about sports or the kids. At nearly every job I've had, the camraderie more than made up for the long hours and heavy workload. Today, however, a lot of people are stuck behind computers and never have the occasion or inclination to interact with coworkers except by e-mail. That's a shame. It's those casual encounters—hand-delivering some statistics a colleague needs for a presentation, stopping to ask someone if his wife is over the flu, schmoozing at the photocopying machine—that cement the human-to-human connections that make workplace interactions smoother and more enjoyable. We go out of our way to help people we know and like, and those offline conversations are key in building rapport.

Office romances are in a different category than friendships. Some companies have policies against spouses working together, but they can't legislate against couples who aren't married to one another. The issue with any couple is how they handle their relationship at work. I worked in the same office with two people for almost two years before I found out they were married. They were assigned to different departments, and when we had joint meetings, there was nothing to suggest that their relationship was more than collegial. I'm told their marriage even went through a rough patch during the time I worked with them, but you would never have guessed it from their professionalism during office hours.

Other people aren't so self-contained. I know one couple who met and moved in together while they were working side by side. Not only were their colleagues able to follow the ups and downs of the relationship on a daily basis, but when the relationship ended most of the office felt obliged to take sides. Many companies discourage such unions for just these reasons: relationships can be a distraction when conducted under the watchful eyes of colleagues, and it's difficult for everyone, not just the couple, if they break up. In general, it's probably best not to know all the gritty details of coworkers' lives. On the other hand, people who are warm and forthcoming often garner a lot of goodwill and support from their colleagues. If they're also capable, that can bump them ahead of less personable coworkers when promotions are being handed out.

How companies handle employee frustration is telling. An angry outburst might provoke immediate dismissal from some organizations, while in others, a more compassionate leader would try to get the backstory on what's going on with the disgruntled worker. There may be a legitimate concern within the company to which the employee is reacting, albeit inappropriately. Empathy and deft listening skills can often defuse a volatile situation and turn it into a learning opportunity.

Sensitivity to other people and the ability to walk in their shoes are key skills for managers who have to lay off staff—which is just about anybody in today's market. There are bosses who assemble the whole team and spell out why layoffs are necessary while showing compassion for what laid-off employees will face. That sort of openness and consideration is a far cry from firing someone behind closed doors, then giving her fifteen minutes to clear her desk before being escorted from the building. Parting from a company and coworkers, especially if you've worked there for much of your career, is often as difficult as leaving a marriage. An empathic boss takes that into account without going overboard in the "I feel your pain" department. Workers want leaders who understand their concerns but also can keep it together well enough to lead.

One psychologist likened empathy in the workplace to Stanislavski's system for actors: if you haven't been through exactly what your employee or coworker is facing, think of something similar you *have* experienced and call up those emotions so you can feel what the other person is feeling.

Then again, thanks to mirror neurons, you may already be feeling what they're feeling in your body, and you just need to tune in to it.

Given the role of work in most people's lives and the amount of time we spend at the office, getting along with coworkers and treating one another civilly are critical skills. From the kid who delivers the mail on up to the CEO, everyone's personality counts. According to William Baker and Michael O'Malley, the authors of *Leading with Kindness*, qualities like humility, gratitude, humor, and compassion make for effective leaders. Whatever their positions, people who are kind, respectful, pleasant, and interested in others, without being suck-ups or pushovers, will contribute to creating an enlightened workplace.

Unfortunately, there are still executives in the corner office who may be great at operations but sorely lacking in people skills. I once had a boss I called the smoke jumper. Like those daring men who parachute into forest fires, he sprang into action at the first sign of a crisis—a fire to put out. The rest of the time, he was largely unavailable—distracted and seemingly uninterested in what the staff was doing. His skill was fire-fighting; he had no aptitude for fire prevention or team building. He wasn't a psychological pyromaniac, starting fires just to put them out. He didn't have to be. Any company or organization always has plenty of crises to address.

Every company is looking for ways to deliver its product

without compromising the bottom line. Customer service, as we all know, seems to be the first thing to go. How many times have you heard a frontline worker say, "Oh, we tell management, but then nothing happens." Sometimes management is complicit. One of the chain drugstores near where I live is notorious for inattentive clerks and spotty service. But now and then they outdo themselves. One night, the checkout line was at a standstill because both the clerk and the night manager were busy licking popsicles that had turned their tongues a lurid blue. When I asked if someone could check out my items, the manager yelled at me, "Cool it, lady. Can't you see we're busy?" Personally, I find it particularly unsavory and off-putting when clerks eat while they're waiting on customers or ringing up grocery items. But when management becomes part of the problem, and no one is modeling appropriate behavior for the employees, everybody suffers. There's a new day manager in that store who is polite and responsive, but his buttoned-up approach hasn't yet filtered down to the night shift.

What a contrast to companies that put customer service at the top of the list. Zappos, the online shoe store, is one. Not only do they have live people manning the phones, but staff members are encouraged to take the initiative in helping customers. The record length for a customer-service call is five hours and twenty-five minutes—nobody hangs up on customers who just need to talk. Kindness is also part of the in-house culture. One community-building initiative is the Random Acts of Kindness Parade: three employees chosen randomly by their peers are showered with attention and appreciation for a day.

We seem to be living in schizophrenic times as far as the workplace goes. On the one hand, we're inconvenienced and insulted every day by personnel who have no clue what service means. On the other hand, we have companies in which the brass are committed to bringing human values to the workplace. Change in the right direction begins with the individual. As consumers, when we are badly served, we need to register our complaints at as high a level as possible. And as workers we can do our part by being proactive and enthusiastic, sensitive to the company's goals as well as our coworkers' well-being. Then maybe one of these days—say, 2019—night clerks will no longer need to eat blue popsicles on the job.

Chapter Seven

··· ━ ···

Digital Life

Turning on TV news one night, I heard a correspondent introducing a story on texting. Here's the segment as it unfolded: A young teen is sitting at a table, hunched over her cell phone, thumbs flying. Across the table, doing exactly the same thing, is a forty-something woman who could be the girl's mother. Oh, wait—she is the girl's mother. The two are at home, seated face to face over their dinner table. Off camera, we hear the correspondent, incredulous, asking the girl, "Are you texting your *mother*?!" *Pause.* "Why don't you just *talk* to each other?" The girl laughs sheepishly. The camera cuts away before we see the mother's reaction.

This is life today—a scene repeated in homes all across America. Youngsters age eighteen and under spend some eight hours a day using their electronic gadgets—the equivalent of eleven hours if you consider that during some of those eight hours they're multitasking on more than one gadget. The latest research shows that the average teen sends or receives some 3,340 texts a month—more than one hundred a day. (Make that five hundred texts a day for one Bronx eighth grader.) But it isn't only kids who are glued to their smart phones. Parents are just as guilty. Many are mouthing, "Do as I say, not as I do," even as they tell their kids to put away their devices, at least at meals. Now, in a twist, it's often the kids who are pleading with their parents to put down the phone and pay attention to them. You know the parents I mean—maybe you are one. "Mom! Mom! Mom!" the toddler wails, twisting around in her stroller while Mom, oblivious, giggles into the cell phone pressed to her ear, or taps out a text message with her free hand. "Dad, watch me!" the Little Leaguer shouts, but Dad, the ubiquitous Bluetooth headset hooked over his ear, has retreated to the far end of the bleachers to field a call.

Perhaps nobody knows better how kids like this feel than clinical psychologist Sherry Turkle. Director of the Initiative on Technology and the Self at the Massachusetts Institute of Technology, Turkle spent five years interviewing children to see how their parents' technology use affected them. The results were not pretty. Again and again, children expressed their hurt that their parents were ignoring them at mealtimes, in the car after school, and at their sporting events.

The kids aren't alone in their frustration, however. Adults who are fed up with being on the receiving end of the fractured attention of their texting, tweeting, blogging, cell phone–toting friends and colleagues are starting to push back against the tide of technology-related rudeness. How many times have you sat down to a meal with friends or colleagues and the first thing they do is pull out their BlackBerries and iPhones and plunk them down on the table? Then, throughout the meal, they keep sneaking sidelong glances at the screen, checking to see who's calling, who called, who might call, who texted. "Mmm? What did you say?" they ask distractedly, as they reluctantly pry their eyes away from their phones. Unless you're doing the same thing—shame on you if you are—you'll probably find the meal frustrating and curiously unsatisfying.

Social media are here to stay. That's a fact. It's no use wishing otherwise. And of course there are advantages galore to cell phones and the Internet with all its attendant technology—they've made life easier, safer, and more efficient in more ways than we can count. We can find lost friends, stay connected at a distance, conduct business anywhere in the world, and run our entire lives remotely if we wish. It's safe to say that technology and social networking have transformed everything about life in the twenty-first century—especially how we relate to one another. But is the new *nice* simply to put up and shut up—or join them—when people text at the dinner table, check Facebook at the movies, look at sports scores during business meetings, interrupt squash games to tweet, and carry on loud, lengthy, intimate cell phone conversations in elevators, on the bus, at the opera, and walking down the street? This may be everyday life today, but that doesn't mean it's nice. Not by a long shot.

And we haven't even mentioned e-mail. Daniel Goleman, author of the bestsellers *Emotional Intelligence* and *Social Intelligence*, started off a column in *The New York Times* with the following anecdote:

> As I was in the final throes of getting a book into print, a woman at my publisher sent me an e-mail that stopped me in my tracks. I had met her just once, at a meeting. We were having an e-mail exchange about some crucial detail, which I thought was being worked out well. Then she wrote: "It's difficult to have this conversation by e-mail. I sound strident and you sound exasperated."
>
> I was shocked to hear that I sounded exasperated. But once she had named this snag in our communications, I realized that, indeed, there was something really "off." So we had a phone call that cleared everything up in a few minutes, ending on a friendly note. . . .
>
> Face-to-face interactions are information-rich; we pick up how to take what someone says to us not just from their tone of voice and facial expression, but also their body lan-

guage, pacing, as well as the synchronization with what we do and say. Most crucially, our brain's social circuitry mimics in our neurons what's happening in the other person's brain, keeping us on the same wavelength emotionally.

Try to do that with a couple of emoticons and an LOL. It just doesn't work.

Here are those mirror neurons kicking in again—the social circuitry we read about in the previous chapter. Social networking gives us the feeling we're in touch—close touch, maybe even hourly or minute-to-minute touch—but it will never be the same as communication face to face, or even voice to voice. There's no way to simulate in a few lines of text the social cues Goleman mentioned. Have you ever watched a TV interview with the sound off? Try this with Charlie Rose. If the conversation is going well and both parties are in some accord, you will probably see them gradually synchronize their movements—hand gestures, crossing their arms or legs, even brushing away a lock of hair. And then if you turn up the sound, you will probably hear them begin to match each other's speech in cadence and volume. (Next time you're talking with someone, notice your own posture and voice, and the other person's.) Give me a few minutes on the phone with an editor friend in England, and I slip into a British accent. It's not that I have a great ear for accents, either. Thanks to our brain-based tendency to mimic—how else do you think we learn language as toddlers?—this sort of synchronization can happen to everyone. Texting and e-mail, by stripping away visual and aural cues, leave us dependent on the written word to convey nuances of meaning. With 140-character tweets and text messages that read "u cn pk me up @4," opportunities for eloquence are nonexistent. And as messages fly back and forth as fast as the fingers can move, forget the thoughtful, reasoned reply. As for humor—and the warm glow of shared laughter that makes our brains light up with pleasure—forget that, too. However much your teenager will insist that everything she and her friends are texting is *HA HA HA,* a riot, humor is largely lost in the cloud.

At bottom, social networking is just our gadgets talking to one another. And as attached as we are to them—even anthropomorphizing them at times—as yet none of those gadgets has a heart or a soul or a brain with the social circuitry that Dan Goleman described. If we're wired to connect, social networking makes sure we don't get *too* close. I can post photos from the latest beer blast or family trip—with some snarky captions—on my Facebook page, and it's the next best thing to your having been there, right? Not really. Furthermore, we've all heard the horror stories about people

If we're wired to connect, social networking makes sure we don't get too close.

being bullied or stalked or fired because of injudicious words and pictures they posted online.

There is something about the pseudo-intimate, house-of-mirrors hyperreality of social networking sites that disinhibits us in about the same way as a bottle of wine—sometimes with more disastrous results. Assuming you don't get arrested for drunk driving or say something outlandish to the boss's wife, you can always sleep off the wine. But that angry e-mail, indiscreet Facebook profile, and just-this-side-of-libelous blog post may be harder to sleep off. We think of Facebook posts, text messages, e-mails, and tweets as tossed-off, ephemeral jottings, but the fact is, they're here forever—or at least until software developers come up with the promised technology to make electronic data self-destruct. For now, it's our reputations that are at risk of self-destructing if we're careless with social media. Of course, online misbehavior doesn't always end badly—which is why we keep doing it. But put us in front of a screen and anything can happen. Just as it's easy to go ballistic on the telephone when we're frustrated over customer service gone wrong, even nice, well-adjusted people can let fly in a text or e-mail when somebody doesn't do what they want.

That said, the "online disinhibition effect," as it's called, that can turn us into flamers has an upside as well. John Suler, a psychologist at Rutgers University who studies online behavior, noted that the Internet can also make us more self-revealing in a good way, allowing us to share feelings and fears, wishes and dreams that we might be too shy or self-conscious to disclose in face-to-face encounters. Furthermore, he adds, people may "show unusual acts of kindness and generosity, sometimes going out of their way to help others." A young woman I know who balked at joining a twelve-step group in her neighborhood found fellowship and support by "attending" meetings online. Just as there are chat rooms, message boards, and blogs for nearly every possible interest, there are chat rooms, message boards, and blogs for every conceivable illness or disorder. One good—dare I say *nice*—thing about social media: we don't have to go through anything alone anymore.

But maybe that's not all good. The ability to be alone without being lonely is a station on the road to maturity. Increasingly, we don't seem to be willing to be without digital companionship for even a second, whether we're walking down the street, in the shower, or dressing to go out with friends. Nowadays the first thing many people do when they wake up in the morning is roll over and check their cell phones. You never know who might have sent a text or a funny photo overnight from some distant time zone.

Social media have changed the way we interact with one another, raising questions about what's nice. What are the rules now? With YouTube videos going viral in hours, we need to give more than a passing thought to what's kind and polite versus what's prurient and intrusive. Teen-on-teen cyber-bullying has gotten lots of press—sadly it has even led to suicides. But adults aren't immune to having their humiliating moments put up for ridicule. Think of that YouTube video of the woman falling headfirst into a fountain while walking and texting—she tried to sue to have it removed after it got over two million hits. It's understandable why she found the video so embarrassing: for one thing, the fountain is in the middle of a shopping mall where the woman works! And the fact that it was accessed by so many people suggests that it aroused the collective schadenfreude: I *would never be that stupid*, we were thinking as we watched, laughed, and saved it in our "Favorites" queue to laugh at again and again and again. What's important to remember, however, is that any of us could be that woman. Talking or texting while walking can be hazardous—never mind annoying to anyone we plow into because we aren't looking—and phoning or texting while driving can be fatal, as we've seen. Despite laws against it, the problem has become so widespread that Oprah launched a "No Phone Zone Pledge." Anyone signing it makes a commitment to "end distracted driving" by not texting or making phone calls while behind the wheel. It should be obvious why making a commitment like this is more than nice—it's the decent thing to do if we care at all about other people. Sometimes we forget that using the technology that allows us to network is a social act in itself. Nice people don't do things that could jeopardize the safety and well-being of others.

Cell phones are so ubiquitous that it's almost impossible to arrive at any consensus on the etiquette of their use. Cell phone *misuse*, however, was high on the list of what our Nice Survey participants considered not nice. As Mary Landers observed, "Talking on a cell phone when entering a building or while going through the checkout line at a store seems so emblematic of how little we revere the stranger as a human being. We can start being nice to one another simply by being aware of each other's presence."

Recently I read a newspaper column written by a psychiatrist, describing various ways her patients handle calls they receive during a session. For the most part, she was in favor of "closing out the world," she said, in order to better "grasp the complexity of an individual's mind." But if the patient does take the call, the call itself may become the topic of discussion, which can be very revealing, she added. But how about this as a new rule: unless you're a physician on call, why not just turn off the phone for the fifty minutes you're in the therapist's office—or in any doctor's or other professional's office, for that matter? It shows respect for the professional's time and expertise (and, incidentally, means you're more likely to get your money's worth out of the visit). One of the biggest challenges we face in a world dominated by social media is being willing to turn the gadgets off.

Few things are nicer than being with someone who doesn't spend the time you are together answering her phone, or checking to see who's calling, or stepping outside to make a call. ("I'll just be a minute" has become the new cliché of interpersonal relations.) Twice over the past decade I've gone without a cell phone for a matter of months. Yes, it can be inconvenient—before cell phones, how did we ever let someone know we were running late, or settle an argument without Google to guide us? But the upside of not having a phone—or, alternatively, of leaving it turned off or at home—is that you're not on call 24/7 and you don't assume others are either. We've become so used to multitasking and distractions that we've forgotten what it feels like to be fully present in the moment, wherever we are, with whomever is right here in front of us. That sort of undivided attention is one of the qualities that's most pronounced in nice people—and most attractive, even to dedicated multitaskers. We love people who pay attention to us, even if we don't return the favor. In fact, social networking can starve us for contact with real people, even those we don't know or know well. Meredith Melnick, a reporter for *Time* Healthland online, established "cell phone-free Sundays" for herself. She did it, she explained, not out of consideration for her nearest and dearest, but because she missed interacting with strangers: in the year since she had acquired her iPhone, she had never been lost and forced to ask directions. That might not be reason enough for most of us to declare a phone-free day—or phone-free zone. But it's one good way to focus on the pleasure we derive from others' company, not their truncated messages or disembodied voices.

In 2010, Reboot, a non-profit think tank of media-savvy Jewish professionals in New York, San Francisco, and Los Angeles, instituted a National Day of Unplugging, which was such a success that they plan to make it a yearly event. From sundown one Friday in March to sundown the next day, all sorts of people who are habitually tethered to their computers and smartphones made a commitment to abide by what Reboot dubbed the Ten Principles:

- Avoid technology
- Connect with loved ones
- Nurture your health
- Get outside
- Avoid commerce
- Light candles
- Drink wine
- Eat bread
- Find silence
- Give back

There's an obvious link here to traditional Sabbath rules, but observing these principles wasn't just eye-opening for the

Jews who participated. A number of Christians, a Muslim, and an atheist or two were also among those posting testimonials on the Sabbath Manifesto website community page set up for the Day of Unplugging. "Amazingly calming," Anna from London, England, observed. "Wholesome, insightful, and refreshing," said Will Sloan, a web designer in Nashville, Tennessee. For many people the Day of Unplugging was clearly the first time they had reflected on what they might be missing by spending so much time on the phone and online. Notably, a number used the day to reconnect with family and friends. In describing his unplugged day for the *Huffington Post*, the actor Josh Radnor, who stars in the TV series *How I Met Your Mother*, wrote, "I saw some friends . . . I rehearsed a wonderful play with some talented folks, I saw my niece and nephew and had a really nice dinner with my sister. Nothing flashy. But it felt real, slower."

Obviously not everyone would be willing or able to unplug for a day. But even those who have reservations could take a step in that direction. The Sabbath Manifesto website offered a limited-edition "cell phone sleeping bag" by Jessica Tully, a conceptual artist, to remove temptation. Product designer Ingrid Zweifel took the notion even farther with "the Phonekerchief," a handkerchief embroidered with the words *My phone is off for you*. The idea is to fold it over a cell phone to make a neat little package that can be placed on the dinner table to signal mealtime companions that they're more important to you than incoming calls. As added insurance against being tempted mid-meal, the Phonekerchief fabric is woven with tiny metal fibers that block cell phone reception. The Phonekerchief was Zweifel's senior thesis at Parsons the New School for Design, and on a now-defunct website launched for the project, she posted a message that captures the conundrum facing social media users today: "We may be sitting at the same table, but we are not together: a common condition of our over-wired world. It is time to question what truly nurtures the human spirit."

These days, not only are we subjected to too much information of all kinds, but with social media our lives seem to have open borders. The ease of dashing off a message—who stops to mull over the contents when something Twitter- or text-worthy is happening?—is a set-up to be too self-revealing. Even in this era of living out loud, there are limits to what we want to—or should—know about each other. We haven't completely forgotten the seduction of a little mystery. Walking the line between tasteless revelation and Garbo-like silence is an essential part of being nice.

It's tempting to think that privacy is just an illusion. After all, the social circuitry in our brains makes our actions and intentions transparent to each other—at least if we're paying attention. But perhaps the fact that we *are* irretrievably linked to one another is reason enough to be more, not less respectful of personal boundaries. To that end, it's a relief to know that our innermost thoughts are not always an open book. Some researchers suggest that in addition to mirror neurons, we have "super" mirror neurons that inhibit the tendency to imitate others' behaviors or pick up on their intentions. (If we didn't have some way of shutting off the noise, we would be in perpetual emotional turmoil, buffeted about by all the distractions.) But we've gotten so used to reporting the minutiae of our lives on social media that the idea that some of it might be out of bounds seems inconceivable. We have even reached the point when hostesses have to warn their guests, "Please don't tweet this conversation." (Another rule: unless it's your party, resist the urge to post a photo you snapped with your iPhone—at least until after you get home.)

It's hard today to keep anything private, even for the 99.9 percent of us whose lives aren't routinely covered in *People*. It used to be, for example, that when you got engaged you would quietly share the good news with family and a few chosen friends, then make a formal announcement in the newspaper to inform the world. But now, you've barely said yes before somebody who overheard somebody whose sister works for the jeweler from whom your fiancé bought the ring has already spread the word in a tweet that went out to five thousand of your neighbors. The speed with which news, good or bad, travels, leaves it up the individual to draw the line.

Discretion and restraint are qualities nice people take to heart. Not everyone is paparazzi fodder, but still there are unexpected consequences to letting social media run your life.

Emily Gould was twenty-four when she launched her blog, Emily Magazine. What began as a way to stay in touch with old friends—don't they all?—and a small circle of new online friends, became increasingly problematic as the blog was folded into Gawker, and Gould's revelations took on a kind of *Sex and the City* life of their own. With the attention came the posturing—an online persona that was increasingly manufactured as the events and people she wrote about veered away from the unpretentious anecdotes she once told. Social media make it easy to be someone we're not. We don't have to create an avatar on Second Life: we can reshape our original selves into an identity that's close enough to the real one to be recognizable but has none of its nicks and dings. After embracing Twitter with a vengeance, writer Peggy Orenstein praised "its infinite potential for connection, as well as its opportunity for self-expression," at the same time she had nagging doubts. The questions about social media she raised are those that any thoughtful—OK, I'll say it again: nice, decent, kind—person might raise:

> *When every thought is externalized, what becomes of insight? When we reflexively post each feeling, what becomes of reflection? When friends become fans, what happens to intimacy?*

The risk of the performance culture, of the packaged self, is that it erodes the very relationships it purports to create, and alienates us from our own humanity.

Virtual life has made us "virtuosos of self-presentation," Sherry Turkle says. The title of her latest book, *Alone Together: Why We Expect More from Technology and Less from Each Other,* perfectly sums up the oxymoronic state we live in, happier behind our virtual identities because face-to-face communication is "messy" and too much bother. "We'd rather text than talk," Turkle notes. One woman spoke for many in explaining why she doesn't like talking on the phone: "It's too much work."

It's work that nice people are only too happy to undertake, however. Anticipating a phone call used to be exciting. It might be a lover, a job offer, a coveted invitation, or a favorite aunt calling to see how you are. Now, less than half the cell phone traffic is talking; texting has become the communication of choice.

Instead of those long, delicious phone calls that fed close friendships, now we track one another's comings and goings in text messages and tweets and on Facebook. Anthropologist and evolutionary psychologist Robin Dunbar argues that gossip's social value is critical, going back to early man. At its best—not as fuel for character assassination—gossip "is the core of human social relationships," he says. It communicates

valuable information about the world we share: who's sleeping with whom, who's fighting, who's making up, who's in,
who's out, and so forth. Michael Rogers, a columnist for
msnbc.com, suggests that social networking fulfills gossip's
evolutionary role by giving us "an unprecedented ability to
establish the precise nature of relationships," through "limited profiles and privacy settings [that] provide plenty of signals as to who's close and who is closer." But that brings up
another potential minefield a nice person has to navigate.
We're not necessarily in control of what information is circulating about ourselves. Privacy settings only go so far:
personal information may be revealed, often inadvertently,
through other people in our social networks or on photo
sharing sites and the like. (What Rogers doesn't mention is
Dunbar's other main point about gossip: that it was the way
our early ancestors punished "free riders"—people who use
the group's resources without giving anything in return.)

Between 2008 and 2009, the amount of time we spent on
social networking sites increased 83 percent. We've seen how
social media bring the world closer: the more we know about
people in other cultures, the more opportunity we have to
develop feelings of kinship with them. For some people, however, social networking isn't an adjunct to real life, it *is* their
reality. Friends told me about a couple they know whose ava-

tars met on Second Life and began a torrid affair. Offline, the two were married to other people. But soon, online reality took over, the avatars won out, and the couple's real-world marriages fell apart. I'm curious what happened next. Was the reality of "real life" a disappointment? When your avatar can be all you can be and so much more—mine would be a 5'11" supermodel/scientist with green eyes and an IQ of 175— what sort of life can you expect once your avatar/doppel-ganger and your partner's step out from behind the curtain?

How self-revealing should I be? is an age-old question for lovers, at least in the getting-to-know-you stage. But online relationships pose a dilemma we didn't have to face even a decade ago: *How truthful do I have to be?* Authenticity and trust are important strengths of character that we value in others as the foundation of our relationships. Facebook's founder Mark Zuckerberg has insisted from the get-go that people should join Facebook under their real names. Not being able to hide behind anonymity makes us behave bet-ter, he argues. "Having two identities for yourself is an exam-ple of a lack of integrity," he told *The New York Times*. But what kind of impression do we make—or want to make—when we go on social networking sites? Is nice the same online as it is off? For starters, we need to think twice about the Twitter handle or e-mail address we choose. One with sexual innu-endos may seem hilarious in college, but it can come back to haunt you later on, when you're applying for a job.

Like most people, I've had plenty of friend requests from people I've never heard of. Usually they turn out to be friends of friends. But why would I want to have a network filled with people I don't know? There's no guarantee that their posts will be edifying or useful to me, or that I will want to support their causes or attend their gatherings—online or off. Many of us find it hard enough to keep up with our offline friends. Robin Dunbar famously theorized that the maximum number of friends one can reasonably manage is around 150. And those are the people we make an effort to know. If I expand the circle to include my Facebook friends, LinkedIn contacts, and so on, there are that many more people to track. It's easy to log on and scan the latest posts from Facebook friends—I don't have to interact with them or play phone tag, and I can maintain a nonthreatening distance between us. So guess which of my friends are more likely to fall by the wayside? Right—the ones I actually feel close to. When it comes to the people in their lives, nice people are loyal and set priorities. They keep up with the people they care about, and don't try to be everyone's best friend.

And then there's the delicate subject of intimacy and social media. I'm not talking about phone sex or online sex but relating to intimate partners. It's hard to imagine anyone crass enough to propose marriage in a text or e-mail, but all too often we hear of someone getting the heave-ho from a relationship or a job electronically. "Not nice" would be an understatement. But it's amazing what passes for acceptable behavior online that we wouldn't tolerate in real life. There are countless books, websites, blogs, and magazine articles devoted to "e-manners," and no wonder. Although there's some evidence that flame wars are on the downswing, the disinhibition effect mentioned earlier shows no signs of abating. When we're online, Dan Goleman explains, the bit of brain machinery that scans the social scene and monitors our responses isn't receiving cues from the environment as it would if we were face to face, so how we respond may be out of sync. And even when we text or instant-message about events as they happen, we're not really communicating in real time. Who knows when the recipient will pick up the message—or how long he will take to reply. Or what mood he'll be in when he does reply.

Since we're essentially operating in a vacuum online, we can project whatever we want onto the person on the other end. Fantasy may run wild. (At least with a phone call, we have a voice and its nuances to ground us.) Furthermore, as John Suler points out, there are none of society's usual "rules" curbing us online, and no real authority figures. We're all equal, all buddies, so we feel fewer compunctions about what we say.

This doesn't mean that it's the Wild West out there, however. Anyone with a well-developed prefrontal cortex—the part of the brain that modulates emotion and self-control—

can approach social networking responsibly and carry on a balanced and fulfilling life both online and off. More of us are starting to monitor our responses—thinking through a message before we push "send"—although it would be nice if more people would use spell-check. The actor John Cusack, an enthusiastic tweeter, has gotten flack for his garbled messages and inadvertent neologisms. "If you're going to be political, maybe learn how to spell Pakistan, and all words in general," wrote a disgruntled fan. Even some of the celebrity bloggers are becoming kinder: gratuitous negativity is going out of style.

Concern about how social networking is affecting us goes all the way up to the top. In a statement for World Communications Day, addressed to "Brothers and Sisters," Pope Benedict XVI urged us all to attend to the risks as well as the opportunities afforded by new technologies: "In the search for sharing, for 'friends,' there is the challenge to be authentic and faithful, and not give in to the illusion of constructing an artificial public profile for oneself."

There is almost no one these days who isn't connected in some way via social media and social networking. Even your aging grandmother is probably e-mailing her friends right this minute or downloading photos of the grandkids from the iPhone you gave her last Christmas. Holed up for the winter in the weather station on top of Mount Washington, you would be crying for the community of Facebook and

YouTube—not to mention playing chess online, joining a book discussion group, and cruising for dates on Second Life. To manage all this, what's required of us is a modicum of good sense—social and emotional awareness. Nice people don't distinguish online life from life offline in one important sense—they hew to the same standards of kindness, decency, and sensitivity to others.

Ultimately, what it comes down to is that we are first and foremost human beings, not cyborgs, and there is no better place for nice people to meet up than in the company of one another. Online services are popping up to do just that: help people get together IRL—that's Web talk for "in real life." Life online has reached such an extreme that it was inevitable we would begin to yearn for conversations face to face. A couple of years ago, *Monocle*, an upscale magazine of culture and world affairs, ran a "Most Unwanted" column listing five items: number four was Twitter. "There is a kind of social media that really works for business and play," the text said. "It's called having a glass of wine."

Chapter Eight

························ ● ························

Too Nice for Your Own Good

Now that we've broadened the meaning of nice to include qualities like kindness, courtesy, empathy, and generosity, we can dare ask the question: Can we ever be too nice?

The answer is a resounding yes. For women especially, the landscape of nice is littered with outmoded expectations. Being nice can be a trap. From the time women are toddlers, they're told, "Just be nice, dear." In other words, be a good girl. *Don't complain. Don't make waves. Don't draw attention to yourself. Think of others first.* The list goes on. And the imperative to be nice isn't limited to women. Everyone—male or female—has a personal checklist of nice behavior. Chances are, it's yellowing around the edges, a relic of the messages received in childhood from family and society at large. How many times have we curried favor from someone we didn't like or respect, or hung on to a relationship that no longer serves us "just to be nice"?

In my family, the message was "You've been given so much, you must do for others." Nothing wrong there; that sort of pronouncement can spawn a philanthropist. But the subtext was: You must do for others *to the exclusion of yourself.* Don't consider your own needs; that would be selfish.

I had a stepmother with a shoulder the whole neighborhood cried on. She was chicken soup for everyone's soul. Everyone, that is, but her own family. We were *her* shoulders to cry on—a particular challenge in our teen years. To give you an idea what we thought of that burden, many years later, when she went into a retirement home, only one of her four children and none of her three stepchildren visited her regularly. Not nice, but hardly a surprise.

"Too nice" has a million dark sides. And the harm it can cause fans outward in ever-widening circles, from self to family to friends to coworkers to employers—to just about anyone, really, we come in contact with for business or pleasure. Too-nice behavior can even have diplomatic repercussions, leading to misunderstandings on a global scale.

There's a saying in Al-Anon, a twelve-step program for family and friends of alcoholics: "'No' is a complete sentence." People who are too nice often find it hard to say no, even when it would be the most logical or judicious or humane response to a situation; they fear disappointing or angering someone and being rejected. But people who are incapable of turning down an invitation or a request often find themselves in awkward or undesirable or even precarious situations. Psychologist Jo Ellen Grybz, who leads workshops in learning to be less nice, cited a "scarily prevalent issue": the large number of brides—and bridegrooms—who walk down the aisle reluctantly, in tears, because they are too scared or too ashamed to call off the ceremony once the wedding machinery is operating full tilt. How could one possibly disappoint the parents, the wedding planner, the caterer, the guests—never mind the prospective spouse? Even in less fraught situations, I've heard people admit they didn't extricate themselves from a situation that wasn't working because they would "rather be dead than embarrassed."

Sometimes we say yes when we should say no out of concern that someone in authority, the boss perhaps, will find out that we have no idea what we're doing. We can't say no to the boss, we reason, without jeopardizing the job. But isn't it strange how seldom overly nice people stop to think that it's far riskier to take on a project they're not up to than to turn it down in the first place? There are whole books published on how to say no strategically and gracefully so that the needs of everyone involved are met. Sadly, the too-nice person is usually the last to read the advice.

For some people, saying yes is reflexive. It's not only that they want to be seen as likeable and cooperative, they also don't want to miss an opportunity. Behavioral economist Dan Ariely found that when people think they are about to lose their options, they will go to any lengths to keep them open, even if the options themselves aren't all that important to them. One time, a woman told me, "I don't ski, I hate snow, but New Year's is coming, so I said I'd go to Vail with some friends. Then some other friends asked me to join them in Cancun, and since I prefer the beach, I said yes to them. But then I realized I couldn't let down Gran, so I told her I'd stay home and visit her. Now I don't know what to do! Do you think they'll be mad if I change my mind?" Saying yes keeps doors open. The too-nice person may think her motivation is not to disappoint others, but the net effect is just the opposite. A hostess I know dropped several people from her guest list because every time they accepted an invitation from her, they ended up cancelling at the last minute—presumably when something better came along.

Sometimes we say yes to one thing to avoid another. If I agree to go to the ballgame with you, I don't have to lunch with my mother-in-law. But who wins here? My mother-in-law's feelings are hurt because I won't spend time with her, and I'll cast a pall over your afternoon because it's obvious my heart isn't in the game. Worse yet is if I go to the game with you, then sulk in my seat. Even the nicest person acting badly spoils everybody's fun.

Few people provoke more negative—or at least more

conflicted—feelings than compulsive helpers. Much as they want to be kind, their efforts invariably cross a line. These are the people who won't take no for an answer, no matter how much the people around them protest. While ostensibly their intent is beneficent, the result is anything but. It's like the old joke about the Boy Scout who guides an old lady across the street, only to have her say with irritation, "Young man, I was trying to go in the *other* direction." A stereotype of the compulsive helper is the mother who overfeeds her children—and anyone else she can lure to her table.

Food may mean love, but it isn't loving to press others to pack on pounds. There's a Korean horror movie, *301/302*, that illustrates this compulsion in the extreme. A woman hungry for her husband's affection plies him with meals he doesn't want, and when he fails to give her the attention she seeks, she cooks up his beloved dog and serves it to him for dinner—the pet he dearly loved because, unlike his wife, it didn't make demands on him.

A more benign version of the compulsive helper is the compulsive matchmaker. Like Jane Austen's Emma, I went through a romantically meddlesome period that was consistently disastrous. One couple, after a whirlwind courtship, did end up getting married, and for some years I paraded them about as my success story. But a decade later, when the marriage blew apart, nobody was thanking the matchmaker. I was mortified. That was the last time I ever interfered.

There are many motivations behind helping, of course, and compulsive helping may be a mix of several. But for the overly conscientious do-gooder, the urge to serve others runs second to the need for recognition or approval. Being super-nice is a plea for validation. One of the most common pitfalls of too-nice people is thinking that if *they* don't take care of something or someone, no one else will. Delusions of indispensability rapidly devolve into martyrdom. (Think of that poor, put-upon person who steps in to fill the breach left by everybody else.) Doing something out of a sense of duty or obligation can easily backfire, however. We drive away the very people we set out to help because they can't stand the guilt we induce in them with our suffering sighs. Sometimes delusions of indispensability are simply a cover for willfulness or even pathology. There's a popular reality TV series about animal hoarders, in which nearly all the people profiled insist that they have overpopulated their homes with dogs—or cats, or birds, or reptiles—for the animals' benefit when, in reality, the animals are in sorry shape and are about to be removed by the ASPCA.

The too-nice person who is conflict averse will do anything to avoid unpleasantness: say yes, say no, jump through hoops—whatever seems most likely to keep the peace. Here, too, there's a downside. Suppressing what you really think or feel, and not getting your own needs met, builds resentment. Anger is the snake in the room, coiled to strike and spoil whatever good feelings exist in your relationships. Addicts and alcoholics are fond of this strategy: it's an excuse to pick up a drink or a drug, which only makes the situation worse.

Self-abandonment or self-betrayal is the leitmotif of the overly nice. Without a healthy sense of self, it's hard to maintain boundaries. Everyone else's needs, desires, and projections override your own. The urge then is either to assume all responsibility for the other person—or to abdicate any responsibility for yourself. Lacking clear boundaries, the too-nice person wonders, "Who am I really?" Take away the people-pleasing, self-sacrificing, conflict-averse patsy, and what's left? Too-nice people often fail to recognize their own worth.

It doesn't take much to turn the people-pleasing aspect of being nice into a full-blown health hazard. Overly nice people often aren't forthcoming about what really hurts—"the doctor was so busy, I didn't want to take up too much time"—and may be too ready to accept a diagnosis or treatment without fully understanding the doctor's findings. The results can be disastrous. We've all heard stories of people who suffered a heart attack or a stroke on the way home from the hospital or doctor's office. A man I know probably saved his life by speaking openly and at length about his symptoms while he was in the doctor's office. His candor enabled the doctor to grasp the urgency of the problem and send him straight to the emergency room to have a stent inserted in his artery.

Too-nice people don't like to inconvenience others—even people whose job is to respond to a patient's or client's or customer's needs. Don't like the way your lamb is cooked? *Be quiet and eat up, don't make a scene*, your inner parent chides. And whose closet doesn't have an item or two with the price tag still hanging from the sleeve because you couldn't face the clerk at the return desk, demanding, "Why are you returning this? What's wrong with it?" It doesn't occur to us to simply say, "Nothing's wrong. I just don't want it." Too-nice people end up with insurance they don't need, sofas they don't like, and more Girl Scout Cookies than the entire neighborhood could consume. There's an old Yiddish proverb: "Too nice can cost a lot of money."

Repairing a tendency to be overly nice doesn't require brain surgery, even if the habit is ingrained. An upside of the relentless self-improvement thrust of our society is the array of resources available to the terminally timid: nearly every Y and health club offers assertiveness training and/or martial arts. And there are books galore giving ten tips for this, nine steps to that, as well as websites encouraging us to drop the Mr. Nice-guy routine and find our inner nasty. Probably most people won't need to go as far as Martin Kihn, author of *A$$hole: How I Got Rich & Happy by Not Giving a Damn About Anyone and How You Can Too.* Kihn claims to have killed the too-nice urge and honed his edge by joining the National Rifle Association, enrolling in a kickboxing class, yelling at work colleagues, and eating garlic bagels on the subway. At the time, Kihn was an editor at the satiric magazine *Spy*, so we can assume he's exaggerating somewhat. But we needn't question entirely the sincerity of a man who opens his book with the line, "I was the nicest guy in the world—and it was killing me."

Reforming an overly nice tendency doesn't require becoming a commando—or a pain in the neck. The Viet Cong leader Ho Chi Minh supposedly said, "The way to straighten a bent bamboo is to bend it in the opposite direction." It's not clear whether Ho had read Aristotle, but on that point, they were in agreement. The goal is to reach a happy medium between too-nice and nasty. There are many ways to achieve that, mindfulness for one. Mindfulness meditation is one of the most effective methods of paying attention to our thoughts and behavior. In a pinch there is always the tried-and-true technique of taking a deep breath and counting to ten, to avoid straying into the same old minefields.

But all this talk about being too nice begs a question: in a world in which kindness and courtesy seem to be in short supply, isn't "too nice" a forgivable error, and better than the alternative? Maybe so, but let's look at some of the other

Isn't "too nice" a forgivable error, and better than the alternative?

potential pitfalls of niceness. In addition to the health hazards of too much people-pleasing and yea-saying, there is the psychological and spiritual toll. Think of people who always seem to be apologizing—for their behavior, for the weather, for their very existence. To hear them tell it, they can never put a foot right. Imagine how debilitating that sort of self-discounting is; it gradually erodes confidence altogether. There are so many positive attributes that nice people harbor, from kindness, generosity, and warmth to empathy, friendliness, and humor. Ideally, our efforts will be directed at enhancing those qualities, while correcting self-defeating attitudes and behaviors. The bottom line is self-care—attending to basic needs like eating right, sleeping well, getting exercise, and, when necessary, seeking help. People who have difficulty speaking up for themselves can ask a friend to accompany them on doctor's visits, to take notes, if necessary, and to forestall any tendency to downplay their needs.

Who says we have to be nice all the time anyway? As the French playwright Molière observed, "I prefer an interesting vice to a virtue that bores." A little backbone, even some well-placed grumpiness, may be just what a situation warrants. "Without negativity," psychologist Barbara Fredrickson writes in *Positivity*, "you become Pollyanna, with a forced clown smile painted on your face. You lose touch with reality. You're not genuine. You drive others away." One of the Nice Survey participants said it really bothered her when people ignored an obvious problem for so-called "compassionate" reasons. "When there's an elephant in the room, talk about the elephant," she insisted.

A dose of abrasiveness can even have a salutary effect, building character, perhaps, or prompting us to think in new ways. Writing about House, the brilliant but irascible doctor in the eponymous TV series, Mélanie Frappier suggested that his confrontational style—the Socratic method straight up— was more effective in making good diagnosticians out of his residents than letting them coast along on their preconceived assumptions would be. The opposite of too-nice may be nasty, but midway is the province of the mensch, who is steady, secure, and not afraid to speak his mind.

From a tender age we're pressured to say "thank you," but, ironically, people in many parts of the world think Americans say it too often. As Margaret Visser explains in *The Gift of Thanks*, we come off as insincere if we're overly effusive about small courtesies or favors that others don't think warrant such an outpouring. Americans have a similar mistrust of people who say "I'm sorry" too much. Do they really regret their behavior? Does it even call for an apology? Is the apology sincere or a form of manipulation: if I say I'm sorry, you won't be mad at me, right?

Skeptics often see blatantly nice people as phony, to the

point of wondering if they're hiding something. Peterson and Seligman suggest in *Character Strengths and Virtues* that "their virtuous deeds mask insecurity or even deeper psychopathology." In some cases, those concerns may be justified. Two examples the authors cite are the politician John Edwards and the golf star Tiger Woods—cultural heroes knocked off their pedestals by sexual indiscretion. On the other hand, we are sometimes too ready to write off someone altogether. Just because we fall short in one area doesn't mean we don't have other virtues. "The real sin," Peterson and Seligman suggest, "may not be the obvious one but the failure of authenticity on the part of the sinner."

Hypocrisy can get anyone into trouble, but for overly nice people it is a special trap. We are quick to criticize anyone we think is being less than honest. Authenticity isn't a small matter. People may not always be kind or courteous, but we do look for integrity—a basic core of honesty in their approach to life and dealings with others. Back in the 1800s, a French neurologist named Duchenne identified two kinds of smiles in human beings—one real, the other fake. The genuine, or so-called Duchenne smile, involves contraction of both the *zygomaticus major* muscle, which runs from the cheek to the edge of the lip, pulling up the corner of the mouth, and the *orbicularis oculi*, which tightens the skin around the outside of the eye socket. In the fake smile, only the *zygomaticus major* contracts. Significantly, the muscle that differentiates the genuine smile from the fake, the *orbicularis,* is the muscle that's *not* under our conscious control. So a close observer can unmask the overly nice person who is feigning interest or delight: there's no telltale crinkle around the eyes.

As already discussed in previous chapters, much of our response to others is unconscious, and we pick up viscerally how genuine they are. Even without a smile to go on, we may be able to tell if someone is faking from their voice or body language or, in some cases, the movement of their eyes.

Overly nice people want desperately to be liked, and they will tell you what they think you want to hear, no matter how far it is from the truth. Years ago, I knew a young woman who embellished nearly everything she said. It was obvious to her friends, but no one knew quite how to tell her that she needn't exaggerate for us to think she was interesting. She was likable without any frills.

Being genuinely nice doesn't require trying. It's instinctive, albeit instinct honed by training and practice until it's the first response. Although some people never lose a taste for dissembling, for most of us the urge abates with age. We can still pull out the socially acceptable lie when appropriate— "How nice to see you again, Mr. Congressman"—but we're no longer tempted to curry approval by groveling like Uriah Heep, the unctuous clerk in Charles Dickens's *David Copperfield*. In the end, niceness is a matter of balance. Sometimes that involves blunting the sharper edges of the personality:

the hot-headed learn to be more laid back, the phlegmatic to be more proactive. We practice saying no and dare to be honest. The goal isn't to become someone else, unrecognizable to ourselves or others, but rather to be the best example of who we really are. To the philosopher Lao-Tzu, becoming virtuous wasn't about acquiring anything but about going with the flow. When we're in sync with the Tao—life as it is—being nice isn't a forced march. It's the natural response to people and events as they come and go.

Conclusion

.... ◆ ....

Are We Nice Yet?

We began by looking at *nice* as a word and as an ethical stance—a stand-in for the good. Then we journeyed through *nice* as a multidimensional definition of personality that comes to life in a social context. We considered the role of *nice* in intimate relationships, and its power in the changing culture of work. We examined being nice as the mainstay of etiquette, as well as a counterforce to the excesses of social media, then arrived at the question "Can we ever be too nice?" and concluded that indeed we can. Now that we've reached the end of the book, where do we stand with *nice*? Is its meaning any clearer? Have we rescued it from the dustheap of worn-out words and given it new life? Is *nice* still just a woolly adjective signifying mild approval, or have we put enough meat on its bones to elevate it to a more prominent place in the pantheon of human qualities and behaviors? The goal was to make *nice* respectable. Did we succeed?

When I embarked on the search for the deeper meaning of *nice*, I wasn't sure what, if anything, I would find. Then, too, many people I mentioned the project to were skeptical. Some turned their noses up at the word itself. "*Nice* is meaningless," said my nephew, Lyman Castle. "It's an empty word." Lyman teaches high school, and *nice* is one of two words he forbids his students to use. The other is *good*. I can see his point: he is teaching students to be more precise, more descriptive in their use of language. But chapter 1, A Checkered Past, advances the argument that *good* was a precursor to *nice*, and remains an integral part of what *nice* means today. In one stroke, my nephew seemingly dispatched the premise of the book. Would *nice* survive the challenge?

Lyman's mother also had little use for nice. In one of the last notes I received from her before she died, she wrote, "I have trouble with the word 'nice,' as in 'nice girl.' I guess I prefer kindness." As it happens, the participants in the Nice Survey were in full agreement. Of the sixty adjectives in the survey, *kind* was the one that stood out. Over 90 percent of the survey participants chose kind as a word they closely associated with *nice*.

In the end, it may not matter which word we use. *Nice, kind, compassionate, friendly, thoughtful, attentive, generous,* or any of a good many other adjectives might do. It's not that words are unimportant. But throughout the book I've tried to show that nice isn't a single trait or quality but a way of being—a posture toward life that transcends the meaning of any one word. What is more important than the label itself is what *nice* as a way of being entails. There is an urgency in the culture right now to restore kindness, generosity, compassion, courtesy, and caring to our relations with one another. Bullying, whether by kindergarteners facing off on the playground or political leaders strong-arming their citizens, is no longer a viable means of getting what we want—if it ever was.

To be nice doesn't mean to be a chump, wearing a painted smile and standing down regardless of what happens around us. Cowardice and Panglossian naïveté are not aspects of niceness. Moral courage is. But we don't need to be moral saints, either. There is nothing more off-putting than someone who is holier than thou, who seems to exist at a far remove. Nice people are earthbound and nonjudgmental, rooted in the here and now, not in what ought to be.

What we've learned about *nice* is that it is not an idea that flies solo. Nice is virtually meaningless without a social context. Like the old expression "beauty is as beauty does," we are nice as a function of how we behave with one another. Although being nice may be defined in any number of ways, no one seems to be confused about what it is once they see it in action.

Some years ago, my niece Betsy Castle, a community and environmental activist who lives in Idaho with her husband and two young daughters, undertook something unusual. She walked across America. When I first heard about her plans, her mother explained it as a walk to publicize the plight of the salmon, which were disappearing from the rivers of the Northwest as logging destroyed their spawning grounds. While preparing this book, I asked Betsy if she had any examples of niceness to contribute. She sent me an essay about her walk. When I read it, I realized that her walk hadn't been just about the salmon. It was a classic journey of transformation. The paragraphs she sent are a parable for our times: what niceness looks like on the ground. Betsy titled her thoughts "Carried Across America."

I had the rare experience of spending nineteen months finding out just how nice people in America can be. In 1995, I set off on a cross-country hike that started in Seattle, Washington, and ended in Cape Henlopen, Delaware. I had been dreaming of this adventure on and off for twenty years and finally decided it was time to go and see what this country was all about. My career at that time was very people-intensive, and frankly, I was ready to be alone for a while. With my golden retriever, Malcolm—and from time to time, various friends who dropped in—I walked through every season, and covered 3,200 miles to reach the Atlantic Ocean.

When I left Seattle, I had only one definite place to stay, with my mother's cousin in Cincinnati, Ohio. I figured I would probably meet a few kind people along the way who would take me in. But as a woman, I was very apprehensive about strangers and my safety.

I set off with Malcolm, and we had only been walking three days when it all began. A woman who lived in an intentional community invited us to stay with her, and from there, as it would continue across fifteen states, I was passed along between friends who had friends in the next town, or between teachers whose classes I had come to talk to. People invited me to stay in their homes, in their churches, and in their barns. People gave me small amounts of money for food and hired me—and anyone walking with me at the time—to do odd jobs. People cooked beautiful, elaborate meals for us, and sent us on our way with whatever we needed at the time. Motel owners in Colorado put us up for free when it was 28 degrees below zero and too cold to camp. People mailed our belongings on to the next town for us. Others rearranged their schedules to take us sightseeing: Yellowstone Park to see the Buffalo; rafting down the Salmon River in Idaho; horseback riding in West Virginia, where we rode into the middle of a pack of new foals grazing in chest-high grass.

My husband, whom I met while I was walking through Idaho, came to walk with me in Kentucky. He flew into Louisville, a large city, and on the first night, as we cleared the

city limits and began to walk through the rolling hills, a mini-
van pulled over in front of us, and a middle-aged woman on
her way to soccer with her three kids rolled down her win-
dow and handed me two twenty-dollar bills: she said she
wanted us to know that Kentucky folks will go out of their
way to help others. That same night we came upon a church,
and when we went in to ask if we could stay the night, three
older women came forward and told us to grab a plate and
join them for their Harvest Party.

Meanwhile, back home in Seattle, I had a wonderful
friend who sold T-shirts to support my walk, collected other
donations, and basically kept us going for over a year and a
half. I believe that it is people's natural inclination to open
their hearts and give, and in walking across America, I
learned that the desire to be kind and help others was strong
enough to pull people out of their comfort zone and take a
chance on us.

Not everyone who sent me their experiences for the book
had as dramatic a tale as Betsy's, but their stories were filled
with the kindness of strangers, and the generosity of family
and friends. Kindness and generosity are measured not just in
cross-country walks but also in modest, everyday encounters.
For all the many qualities niceness seems to encompass, it ultimately represents the triumph of the small—it takes remarkably little of it to turn someone's day, or even life, around.

A writer friend e-mailed me something about the neighborhood market where he and his wife regularly shopped before their recent move. He preferred not to be identified, which is a shame, as he's one of the nicest people I know. His simple tale reinforces the idea that emotions are contagious—and that caring, considerate people are rewarded in kind.

> *While chatting about garlic with one of the sisters who runs the store, I mentioned something about how often it's the first ingredient in what I make for dinner, and how long it takes to peel and mince the requisite number of cloves. The next time I went to the store, one of the clerks asked my name, and when I told him, he said he had something for me from one of the owners. He handed me a Ziploc bag filled with frozen garlic that had been sliced into generous (even by my standards), cook-ready portions along a tiny grid.*

A cynic might say, "That shop owner just wants to drum up business." But I don't think that's it. We've grown so accustomed to the impersonality of the places where we live and work and shop that it's easy to forget that there are whole neighborhoods and communities that operate on a currency of care for one another. Both of these stories confirm that. All across America, we can see the same things: when someone's sick, a neighbor sends over soup and picks up her kids at school. When someone dies, the whole town turns out with casseroles and consolation for the bereaved. Lose a job, and everyone rallies to make sure there's food on your table. And when a baby is born, or someone receives a promotion or an award, the entire community celebrates. Big cities may not seem like places that encourage this sort of exchange, but precisely because they are so big and impersonal, people often go out of their way for friends and neighbors—and customers— just as the grocer did for my garlic-loving friend. A large apartment building or complex is really just a vertical village. We may be a little more respectful of our neighbors' privacy than in a small town, but that's largely because we literally live on top of one another.

No matter where we are, people pitch in. Cheryl Chalmers, an actress and community mediator, described a bus trip she took from Newark Penn Station in New Jersey, to Port Authority Bus Terminal in New York during a driving rainstorm. The trip usually takes fifteen minutes, but this time it took a harrowing four hours. First they got lost. "The driver was scared," she recalled. "But it turned out that the woman sitting in front of me drove a bus for a living! And the man sitting next to her knew the back roads through New Jersey, so together the two of them helped the driver make his way to Port Authority. I felt happy to be a part of people helping people."

Being nice doesn't require extenuating circumstances, as we've seen throughout the book. It greases the wheels of every day. Drop a glove or a dollar, and a stranger will dash after you to hand it back. Even when we expect nothing of one another, we are continually—and pleasantly—surprised. Alex Marshall, who traveled all over the world as a press officer for the United Nations Population Fund, still remembers the time he left his laptop in a taxicab in Cairo, never expecting to see it again. The driver, however, went to great lengths to track him down and return it.

Kindness like that is a natural reaction when we're not preoccupied with our own concerns. *Kind* comes from the Middle English word *kynde*, which in turn comes from the Old English word *gecynd*, meaning natural or innate. Both derive from the same root as family and kin. It's human nature to watch out for kin, our own flesh and blood, and just one step from there to caring about family in a broader sense: other people and species that share our planet.

Buddhists say that it is the *lack* of kindness that's unnatural—a habit we acquire out of ignorance, not realizing our oneness with all around us. As we saw in chapter 3, Heaven Is Other People, what we are learning about mirror neurons confirms how closely we are linked to one another, brain to brain. When we demonize anyone as the Other, whether because of race or gender or values or political leanings, we're subverting our natural inclination to be compassionate and caring. Those teenagers who prey on more vulnerable classmates often played with those same children in the sandbox, swapping trucks and Transformers, or hosting tea parties for their Barbies.

As we've seen, niceness doesn't mean sameness—generic, homogenized personalities. Line up any six nice people, and they will probably be nothing alike. Niceness also doesn't mean embracing everyone and everything indiscriminately. We will always have preferences, always have people with whom we disagree. The nicest people are simply those who haven't forgotten our essential kinship as human beings. There's a line often repeated to newcomers in twelve-step programs that suggests the kind of acceptance and inclusiveness that characterizes nice people: "You may not like all of us, but you'll come to love us in a special way, the same way we already love you."

Respect is a big part of being nice, something we don't see enough of these days. In India, people greet one another by bowing and saying, *"Namaste."* It means many things, but essentially, "The divine in me honors the divine in you." President Obama was widely criticized for bowing to King Abdulah of Saudi Arabia, Emperor Akihito of Japan, China's President Hu Jintao, and a joint session of India's Parliament during official visits. "The President of the free world bows to no one," we were told: bowing is a show of weakness, a strategic error. But Obama wasn't making a political statement, he was making a human one—a gesture of respect. A gesture that's understood and appreciated in nearly every culture the world over.

The world is changing. Warmth and friendliness are making inroads. As we saw in chapter 6, When Kindness Goes to Work, even the workplace is changing for the better, as companies begin to see that kindness won't compromise the bottom line. In fact, compassionate leaders improve performance and morale. All things being equal, most of us would rather spend time with someone friendly, considerate, and giving than with a saturnine, self-centered misanthrope. Whether at work or at home or in love, a pleasing personality wins out. Asked how she stayed on an even keel while filming the demanding role of an obsessed, unstable ballerina in *Black Swan*, actress Natalie Portman said, "I think it's important to work your hardest and be as kind as possible to everyone that you work with. That's the goal every day—just keeping focused on that."

Social media sorely test our capacity to be nice, as discussed in chapter 7, Digital Life. But here, too, there is a glimmer of light under the door. We remain glued to our gadgets, but even diehard techies are beginning to yearn for a little face time IRL—"in real life." We're beginning to realize that Facebook friends won't keep us warm on chilly nights or cuddle us in old age. There are now websites springing up whose sole intention is to connect us up in real time, offline. Imagine: good conversation with people you've just met, over lamb tagine and a nice cabernet.

SURVEY: THE NICE REPORT

·· ···◆··· ··

For more information, see thenicereport.net

1. Think of someone who strikes you as especially nice—
   e.g., friend, family member, coworker, service provider,
   famous person living or dead. In one or two sentences,
   explain what it is about the person you find exemplary.

2. Recall an incident you experienced or witnessed (or read
   or heard about) that made you think, "How nice," or
   "Not nice." Briefly describe it. As you reflect back on the
   incident now, how do you feel?

3. What everyday rudeness or thoughtlessness bothers
   you most?_____

   _____

   _____

4. On a scale of 1 to 5, how important do you think good manners are?

_____ 1 (not at all important)

_____ 2 (not very)

_____ 3 (neutral)

_____ 4 (somewhat)

_____ 5 (very important)

5. How would you rate yourself in the manners department?

_____ very polite

_____ polite

_____ average

_____ it depends

6. Which of the following qualities do you most associate with the word "nice," in regard to people? Check as many as apply. Add any words of your own.

- [ ] accepting
- [ ] admirable
- [ ] agreeable
- [ ] altruistic
- [ ] amiable
- [ ] appealing
- [ ] appreciative
- [ ] appropriate
- [ ] attentive
- [ ] attractive
- [ ] average
- [ ] banal
- [ ] bland
- [ ] charming
- [ ] cheerful
- [ ] compassionate
- [ ] considerate
- [ ] conventional
- [ ] courteous
- [ ] cultivated
- [ ] empathic
- [ ] enthusiastic
- [ ] forgiving
- [ ] friendly
- [ ] fun
- [ ] generous
- [ ] gentle
- [ ] good
- [ ] goody-goody
- [ ] gracious
- [ ] happy
- [ ] helpful
- [ ] hospitable
- [ ] insipid
- [ ] kind
- [ ] loving
- [ ] loyal
- [ ] modest
- [ ] moral
- [ ] naïve
- [ ] open
- [ ] optimistic
- [ ] pleasant
- [ ] polite
- [ ] positive
- [ ] respectable
- [ ] sensitive
- [ ] superficial
- [ ] supportive
- [ ] sweet
- [ ] sympathetic
- [ ] tactful
- [ ] tasteful
- [ ] tender
- [ ] thoughtful
- [ ] tolerant
- [ ] trusting
- [ ] trustworthy
- [ ] unexciting
- [ ] warm

NOTES

INTRODUCTION

In a 2010 poll http://www.rasmussenreports.com/public_content/lifestyle/ general_lifestyle/august_2010/69_say_americans_are_becoming_more _rude_less/civilized.

identified twenty-four measurable character strengths Christopher Peterson and Martin E. P. Seligman, *Character Strengths and Virtues: A Handbook and Classification* (Washington, DC: American Psychological Association and New York: Oxford University Press, 2004), 13.

"The key to being a 'real mensch' . . ." Leo Rosten, *The New Joys of Yiddish: Completely Updated*, revised by Lawrence Bush (New York: Crown, 2001), 223.

"somebody good, kind . . ." *Microsoft Encarta College Dictionary*, ed. Anne H. Soukhanov (New York: St. Martin's Press, 2001), 902.

"you would be happy to befriend . . ." "The Art of the Mensch," JewishLink, http:// www.jewishealing.com/theartofthemensch.html.

"A person is a mensch . . ." "The Art of the Mensch," Jewish Link.

"Home is the place . . ." Robert Frost, "The Death of the Hired Man," in *North of Boston*, 2nd ed. (New York: Henry Holt, 1915), 20.

issue headlined "The New Nice" Meredith Bryan, "My Town of Kind!" *New York Observer* (March 1, 2010): 1; 14-15.

"Nice is the New Black" Rita Wilson, "Why Being Nice Is In," *Harper's Bazaar* (March 2010): 331.

"make it through the holidays . . ." Miranda Purves, "The Kindness Project," *Vogue* (December 2009): 304-9.

"I always put anything disagreeable . . ." Jane E. Brody, "Secrets of the Centenarians," *New York Times* (October 19, 2010): D6.

CHAPTER 1—A CHECKERED PAST

"delightful, agreeable . . ." J. A. Simpson and E. S. C. Weiner, *The Oxford English Dictionary*, 2nd ed., vol. 10 (Oxford UK: Clarendon Press, 1989), 386.

since it was introduced in Middle English Louis G. Heller, Alexander Humez, and Malcah Dror, *The Private Lives of English Words* (London: Routledge & Kegan Paul, 1984), 131.

"ich am vn-wis . . ." *The Romance of William of Palerne*, ed. Walter W. Skeat. Trans. from French, c. 1350 (London: N. Trubner, 1867), 25.

"wanton, loose-mannered, lascivious" *OED* 10, 386.

"Nyce she was . . ." Guillaume de Lorris and Jehan de Meung, *The Romance of the Rose*. Rendered into English by Geoffrey Chaucer (New York, Henry Holt, not in copyright), 17-18.

"coy, shy, affectedly modest" *OED* 10, 386.

"maydens at her first weddying . . ." *The Romance of Sir Beues of Hamtoun*, Part I, ed. Eugen Kölbing (London: Kegan Paul, Trench, Trübner, 1885), 148.

"extravagant" or "flaunting" *OED* 10, 386.

"dainty" . . . "too delicate" *OED* 10, 386.

"of so nyce and soo delycate a mynde . . ." Sir Thomas More, *Utopia*. Reprint of 1556 edition, trans. Ralph Robinson (London: Alex Murray & Son, 1869), 87.

"overly refined" *OED* 10, 386.

"O, Kate, nice customs . . ." William Shakespeare, *King Henry V*, V.2.266.

"nice wenches" William Shakespeare, *Love's Labour's Lost*, III.1.9.

"scrupulous" and "unsullied" *OED* 10, 386.

"How comes it to pass . . ." Jonathan Swift, "A Project for the Advancement of Religion and the Reformation of Manners," *The Works of Jonathan Swift*. 2nd ed., vol. 8 (London: Bickers & Son, 1883), 83.

"tasteful"... "pleasing to others" *OED* 10, 386.

"Lovely as was her person..." Ann Radcliffe, *The Mysteries of Udolpho* (New York: Derby & Jackson, 1859), 6.

"frequently somewhat derisive" *OED* 10, 386.

"the nicest book in the world" Jane Austen, *Northanger Abbey* (Boston: Little, Brown, 1903), 128.

"Oh, it is a very nice word..." Austen, 129.

"I have been clearing off..." Charles Dickens, "Letter to Richard Bentley, 29 December 1836," in *The Letters of Charles Dickens*, Vol. I: 1820-1839, ed. Madeline House and Graham Storey (New York: Oxford University Press, 1965), 217.

"There had been a germ of truth..." Edith Wharton, *The House of Mirth* (New York: Scribner's, 1926), 245.

"has been too great a favorite..." *The New Fowler's Modern English Usage*, 3rd ed., ed. R.W. Burchfield (Oxford UK: Clarendon Press, 1996), 521.

"I far prefer silent vice..." www.brainyquote.com/quotes/quotes/a/albert eins148863.html.

"the end and aim of human life" Aristotle, *Aristotle: Selections from Seven of the Most Important Books*. 7th ed., trans. Philip Wheelwright (New York: The Odyssey Press, 1951), 263.

"moral excellence is the product..." Aristotle, 181.

"excess and deficiency" Aristotle, 193.

"the errors to which we are personally prone" Aristotle, 198.

"in the opposite direction..." Aristotle, 198.

"at the right times..." Aristotle, 197-8.

"We may describe friendly feelings..." Aristotle, *Rhetoric*, trans. W. Rhys Roberts (Stilwell, KS: Digireads.com, 2005), 45.

to Cicero, the key virtues Cicero, *De Officiis*. Book I, *Moral Goodness*, vii.21-2; xiii. 41; xv.47. www.stoics.com/Cicero_book.html.

"Waste no more time arguing..." Marcus Aurelius. *Meditations*, trans. Maxwell Staniforth (Penguin, 1964), X.16.157.

"in everything considers righteousness..." Confucius, *The Analects*, XV.17. http://academic.brooklyn.cuny.edu/core9/phalsall/texts/analects.html.

"Virtue is not left . . ." Confucius, IV.25.

"What you do not wish for yourself . . ." Confucius, *The Analects of Confucius*, trans. and intro. Chichung Huang (New York and Oxford: Oxford University Press, 1997), XV.24.

"One should never do that to another . . ." *Mahabharata*, XVIII.113.8.

"This, in brief, is the rule of dharma" *Mahabharata*, XVIII.113.8.

"That which is hateful to you . . ." *Talmud*, Shabbat 31a.

"Cease to do evil . . ." Isaiah 1:16-17, *Holy Bible*, Revised Standard Version (New York: Thomas Nelson, 1952), 529.

Books like *Le Livre* Geoffroy de La Tour Landry, *Le Livre de Chevalier de la Tour Landry*, ed. Anatole Montaiglon (Paris: P. Jannet, 1854).

"It is a rude fashion . . . their nayles" Giovanni Della Casa, *Galateo, of Manners and Behaviours in Familiar Conversation*, trans. Robert Peterson, ed. Herbert J. Reid (Privately printed, 1892), 16-17.

"polite, pleasant . . . something similar" Giovanni Della Casa, *Galateo,* trans. and intro. Konrad Eisenbichler and Kenneth R. Bartlett (Ottawa, Canada: Dovehouse Editions, 1990), 3.

"To avoid envy and to keep company . . ." Baldassare Castiglione, *The Book of the Courtier (Il Cortegiano)*, trans. Sir Thomas Hoby, 1561 (New York: AMS Press, 1967), 55. Quoted passage rendered in modern English by Joan Duncan Oliver.

"Manners, far from being apart . . ." Arthur M. Schlesinger, *Learning How to Behave: A Historical Study of American Etiquette Books* (New York: Cooper Square, 1968), vii.

As a youth, he copied down a list of 110 George Washington, "Rules of Civility & Decent Behavior in Company and Conversation," *Foundations Magazine*, http://www.foundationsmag.com/civility.html.

"Every action done in Company . . ." George Washington, "Rules of Civility."

"If you can, even remember to help . . ." Marcus Porcius Cato ("Censor"), *Disticha Catonis*, II.1. Accessed at http://www.republikanisme.nl/republiek/monosticha-en-disticha.html.

"Bold and arduous Project . . ." Benjamin Franklin. *The Autobiography and Other Writings*, ed. Kenneth Silverman (New York: Penguin, 1986), 91.

"Health or Offspring" Benjamin Franklin, 92.

"Imitate Jesus and Socrates" Benjamin Franklin, 92.

Franklin's catalogue of guidelines Benjamin Franklin, 91-2.

"the power of the littles" Sarah J. Hale, *Manners; or, Happy Homes and Good Society All the Year Around* (Boston: J. E. Tilton, 1868 and New York: Arno Press, 1972), 80.

"It is not the great things . . . beneath their notice" Sarah J. Hale, 80.

"Dress is the index of conscience . . ." Sarah J. Hale, 39.

Erasmus of Rotterdam Norbert Elias, *The History of Manners*, in *The Civilizing Process, vol. 1* (Oxford UK and Cambridge MA: Blackwell, 1994), 62.

"If you have rolls . . ." Tech Prep Classes, *Etiquette–Our Way: A Teen Guide to Appropriate Behavior* (New York: Louis D. Brandeis High School, unpublished), 2.

"Appropriate behavior to shine forth" *Etiquette–Our Way*, 1.

"There is no beautifier . . ." Ralph Waldo Emerson, *The Conduct of Life* (Boston: Houghton Mifflin, 1903; New York: AMS, 1979), 196. Citations are to AMS edition.

"Ethics, the practice of living . . ." Ron Scapp and Brian Seitz, "On Being Becoming," in *Etiquette: Reflections on Contemporary Comportment*, ed. Ron Scapp and Brian Seitz (Albany: State University of New York Press), 3.

"Good manners can replace morals" P. J. O'Rourke. *Modern Manners: An Etiquette Book for Rude People* (New York: The Atlantic Monthly Press, 1989), 5.

CHAPTER 2—NICE DECONSTRUCTED

"Kate is straightforward . . . really classy girl" Allison Pearson, "Citizen Kate," *Newsweek* (April 11, 2011): 36.

"emphasizes modesty, gradualism . . ." David Brooks, "Two Theories of Change," *New York Times* (May 25, 2010): A27.

"Her public persona is sweet . . ." Irene S. Levine, PhD, "Cultivating Your Inner Jennifer Aniston: 9 Characteristics of Likeable People," http://www.the friendshipblog.com/tags/characteristics-likeable-people.

Levine's nine characteristics Irene S. Levine, "Cultivating Your Inner Jennifer Aniston."

Norman Anderson . . . study published in 1968 Norman H. Anderson, "Likableness Ratings of 555 Personality-Trait Words," *Journal of Personality and Social Psychology* 9, no. 3 (1968): 272-79.

2002 study by Jean Dumas and his team Jean E. Dumas, Michael Johnson, Anne M. Lynch, "Likableness, Familiarity, and Frequency of 844 Person-descriptive Words," *Personality and Individual Differences* 32 (2000): 523-31.

A 2001 Australian study Stephen Bochner and Theresa Van Zyl, "Desirability Ratings of 110 Personality-Trait Words," *The Journal of Social Psychology* 125, no. 4 (2001): 459-65.

1972 German study Peter Schönbach, "Likableness Ratings of 100 German Personality-Trait Words Corresponding to a Subset of Anderson's 555 Trait Words," *European Journal of Social Psychology* 2, no. 3 (1972): 327-34.

results of a 1938 study William F. Thomas and Paul Thomas Young, "Liking and Disliking Persons," *The Journal of Social Psychology*. 9 (1938): 169-88.

"new synthesis in moral psychology" Jonathan Haidt, "The New Synthesis in Moral Psychology," *Science* 316 (May 18, 2007): 998.

"nice versus nasty . . ." Jonathan Haidt, 998,

"Scientific psychology is not able to prescribe . . ." *The Encyclopedia of Positive Psychology*, vol. 1, ed. Shane J. Lopez (Hoboken NJ: Wiley-Blackwell, 2009), 136.

"a manual of the sanities" Gregg Easterbrook "I'm OK, You're OK," *The New Republic* (March 5, 2001): 20-3; cited in Christopher Peterson and Martin E. P. Seligman, *Character Strengths and Virtues: A Handbook and Classification* (Washington DC: American Psychological Association and New York: Oxford University Press, 2004), 4.

found that when a capuchin monkey Frans de Waal, *The Age of Empathy: Nature's Lessons for a Kinder Society* (New York: Harmony Books, 2009), 112-13.

"broaden and build" Barbara Fredrickson, "The Role of Positive Emotions in Positive Psychology," *American Psychologist* 56, no. 3 (March 2001): 218.

Oddly enough, the pleasure we receive Adam Phillips and Barbara Taylor, *On Kindness* (New York: Farrar, Straus and Giroux, 2009), 10.

kindness is the "universal remedy" Piero Ferrucci, *The Power of Kindness: The Unexpected Benefits of Leading a Compassionate Life* (New York: Jeremy P. Tarcher/Penguin, 2007), 12.

"a language which the deaf . . ." Mark Twain, www.thinkexist.com.

Cann was only twenty-three Street Soccer USA, www.streetsoccerusa.org.

"fundamental techniques in handling people" Dale Carnegie, *How to Win Friends and Influence People*, rev. (New York: Pocket Books, 1981), vii.

In a section entitled "Six Ways . . ." Dale Carnegie, 51.

"If we want to make friends . . ." Dale Carnegie, 60.

Jim and Dylan, two men who live Sarah Klein, "Did He Leave a Forwarding Address? Yes, the North Pole," *New York Times* City Room blog (December 24, 2010), http://www.cityroom.blogs.nytimes.com/2010/12/24/did-he-leave-a-forwarding-address-yes-the-north-pole/.

"I can't fix all the world's problems . . . I love that about you" Tom Mason and Sarah Klein, *Miracle on 22nd Street*, Redglass Pictures, video posted on *New York Times* City Room blog (December 24, 2010), http://www.cityroom.blogs.nytimes.com/2010/12/24/did-he-leave-a-forwarding-address-yes-the-north-pole/.

"the master aptitude" Daniel Goleman, *Emotional Intelligence: Why It Can Matter More Than IQ* (New York: Bantam Books, 1995), 78.

Peterson and Seligman describe temperance Peterson and Seligman, 442.

Hugh McDonald, who proved Dan Barry, "Keeping His Hands on Wheel . . . and on Bow, and Strings," in *City Lights: Stories About New York* (New York: St. Martin's Press, 2007), 111-13.

Hollywood star Drew Barrymore http://www.drewbarrymore.com; "Drew Barrymore," *Inside the Actors Studio*, episode 9.11, season 9 (Bravo, March 2, 2003).

child star at seven Interview with Anderson Cooper, *60 Minutes*, CBS News, aired October 18, 2009. Accessed at http://www.cbsnews.com/2102-18560_162-5386795.html?tag=contentMain;contentBody; "Drew Barrymore Biography," People.com, http://www.people.com/people/drew_barrymore/biography.

drinking, drugging . . . Anderson Cooper, *60 Minutes*.

on her own by age fifteen Anderson Cooper, *60 Minutes*.

nude for Interview and Playboy *Interview* (July 1992); *Playboy* (January 1995).

formed a production company . . . http://www.drewbarrymore.org/drew_barrymore/biography.

face of Cover Girl and Gucci www.drewbarrymore.org/drew-barrymore/biog
 raphy.

"Forgiveness is not a question . . ." His Holiness the Dalai Lama, foreword to
 Forgiveness: A Time to Love & A Time to Hate, by Helen Whitney (Campbell
 CA: Fast Pencil, 2011), ix.

"What do you prefer . . ." Helen Whitney, *Forgiveness,* 149.

"This character strength is a quiet one . . . speak for themselves" Peterson and
 Seligman, 435.

"Those who are modest . . ." Peterson and Seligman, 435.

we value it "if not always in ourselves . . ." Peterson and Seligman, 436.

"My interest in science is simply . . ." *The Last Journey of a Genius* (1988), directed
 by Christopher Sykes. BBC-TV production in association with WGBH Boston. Aired on *NOVA,* PBS (January 24, 1989).

"great and original creative ability" *Webster's New World Dictionary of American
 English,* 3rd college edition (New York: Macmillan, 1994), 563.

"the fun of having an adventure" *The Last Journey of a Genius.*

"Courage is something we want . . ." Natalie Angier, "Searching for the Source
 of a Fountain of Courage," *New York Times* (January 4, 2011): D1.

"Emily demonstrated to all . . ." Obituary, *New York Times* (April 16, 2010): A19.

"We love heroes because . . . need to be challenged" Sharon Jayson, "Study: 20%
 of Americans Have Done Heroic Deeds," *USA Today* (January 14, 2011).
 Accessed at http://www.usatoday.com/yourlife/mind-soul/doing-good/
 2011-01-14-heroes14_ST_N.htm.

"Heroes are really the soul . . ." Sharon Jayson, *USA Today.*

"Subway Samaritan" Robin Shulman, *Washington Post* (January 5, 2007).
 Accessed at http://www.washingtonpost.com/wp-dyn/content/article/
 2007/01/04/AR2007010401756_pf.html.

"I just saw someone who needed help" Cara Buckley, "Man Is Rescued by
 Stranger on Subway Tracks," *New York Times* (January 3, 2007). Accessed
 at http://www.nytimes.com/2007/01/03/nyregion/03life.html.

"I felt like jumping . . . like a child" Jonathan Haidt, "The Positive Emotion of
 Elevation," *Prevention & Treatment* 3, article 3 (March 7, 2000): 3.

"Gratitude is a gift ... or love" André Comte-Sponville, *A Small Treatise on the Great Virtues: The Uses of Philosophy in Everyday Life* (New York: Metropolitan Books, 2001), 134.

"Gratitude can never diminish ... onlookers" Peterson and Seligman, 524.

"First, let us reflect ...." "The Five Reflections," *Sutra Book* (New York: The Zen Studies Society, 1982), 29.

"The thing with feathers"; "keeps us warm" Emily Dickinson, "'Hope' is the thing with feathers," in *The Poems of Emily Dickinson: Reading Edition*, ed. R.W. Franklin (Cambridge MA: Belknap Press of Harvard University Press, 1999), 314.

"With hope, we become energized ..." Barbara L. Fredrickson, PhD, *Positivity: Groundbreaking Research Reveals How to Embrace the Hidden Strength of Positive Emotions, Overcome Negativity, and Thrive* (New York: Crown, 2009), 44.

"You see things; and you say, 'Why?' ..." George Bernard Shaw, *Back to Methuselah*. Part I, Act 1. Accessed at www.readbookonline.net/read/12499/30593.

"Courage is not the absence ..." Richard Stengel, "Mandela: His 8 Lessons of Leadership," *Time* (July 21, 2008): 44.

"Lead from the back ..." Richard Stengel, 44.

"Know your enemy ..." Richard Stengel, 46.

the South African leader "is not and never has been ..." Richard Stengel, 48.

"someone who successfully developed his moral reasoning" Peterson and Seligman, 391.

"We learn to be faithful ... standard" André Comte-Sponville, 26.

"ubiquitously recognized and valued" Peterson and Seligman, 13.

"comfortable in saying that someone ..." Peterson and Seligman, 13.

Research shows that "frenemies" Kirsten Weir, "Fickle Friends," *Scientific American MIND* (May/June 2011): 14-15.

"We look at a person ..." Solomon E. Asch, "Forming Impressions of Personality," *Journal of Abnormal and Social Psychology* 41 (1946): 258.

"Such a phenomenon could best be described ..." Richard Nisbett and Timothy DeCamp Wilson, *Journal of Personality and Social Psychology* 35, no. 4 (1977): 250.

"She is as good and caring..." Bill Carter and Brian Stelter, "A New Host is Chosen for 'Today'," *New York Times* (May 2, 2011): B7.

"As a child when I learned..." Bill Carter and Brian Stelter, B7.

applying the kind of "moral algebra" Benjamin Franklin, *The Writings of Benjamin Franklin*, vol. 5, ed. Albert Henry Smyth (New York: Macmillan, 1906), 437.

Webster's definition of nice *Webster's New World Dictionary of American English*, 914.

"Only connect!" E. M. Forster, *Howards End* (New York: Alfred A. Knopf, 1921), 214.

CHAPTER 3—HEAVEN IS OTHER PEOPLE

"There's no need for red-hot pokers" Jean-Paul Sartre, *No Exit*, in *No Exit and Three Other Plays* (New York: Vintage, 1949), 1.

"Hell is—other people," Sartre, 1.

"Into whatever I say about myself..." quoted by Clayton Morgareidge, Clark University. Accessed at http://legacy.lclark.edu/~clayton/commentaries/hell/html; Kirk Woodward, additional commentary. Accessed at http://rickon theater.blogspot.com/2010/07/most-famous-thing-jean-paul-satre.html.

80 percent of our waking hours Nicholas Emler, "Gossip, Reputation, and Adaptation," in Robert F. Goodman, *Good Gossip* (Lawrence KS: University Press of Lawrence, 1994), 122.

between six and twelve of those hours Nicholas Emler, 125.

"We are wired to connect" Daniel Goleman, *Social Intelligence: The New Science of Human Relationships* (New York: Bantam, 2006), 4.

The social circuits ... ever ready to act" Daniel Goleman, *Social Intelligence*, 67.

literally reshapes our brains Daniel Goleman, *Social Intelligence*, 5.

"From the moment of our birth..." Cornelia Bargmann, "The Social Brain," *Charlie Rose*, TV show, aired on PBS (January 19, 2010).

"All emotions are social ... drive our emotions" Richard Davidson, quoted in Daniel Goleman, *Social Intelligence*, 83.

How is it that we feel what others are feeling Vittorio Gallese, Christian Keysers, and Giacomo Rizzolatti, "A Unifying View of the Basis of Social Cognition," *Trends in Cognitive Sciences* 8, no. 9 (September 2004): 396-403.

empathy—the ability to feel Daniel Goleman, *Social Intelligence*, 58.

This ability to understand and experience others' emotional states Marco Iacoboni, Istvan Molnar-Szakacs, Vittorio Gallese, Giovanni Buccino, John C. Mazziotta, and Giacomo Rizzolatti, "Grasping the Intentions of Others with One's Own Mirror Neuron System," *PLoS Biology* 3, issue 3 (March 2005): 529-35.

mirror neurons were first discovered Marco Iacoboni, *Mirroring People: The Science of Empathy and How We Connect with Others* (New York: Picador, 2009), 9-21; Daniel Goleman, *Social Intelligence*, 43.

Not everyone in the scientific community is convinced Ilan Dinstein, Cibu Thomas, Marlene Behrmann, and David Heeger, "A Mirror Up to Nature," *Current Biology* 18, no. 1 (January 8, 2008): R13-R18; Angelika Lingnau, Benno Gesierich, and Alfonso Caramazza, "Assymetric fMRI Adaptation Reveals No Evidence for Mirror Neurons in Humans," *Proceedings of the National Academy of Sciences USA* 106, no. 24 (June 16, 2009): 9925-930.

how contagious emotions are Daniel Goleman, *Social Intelligence*, 13-20.

"neural WiFi" Daniel Goleman, *Social Intelligence*, 38.

"this emotion is reflected in very real physiological changes . . ." Dacher Keltner, "The Compassionate Instinct," in *The Compassionate Instinct: The Science of Human Goodness.* ed. Dacher Keltner, Jason Marsh, and Jeremy Adam Smith (New York: W.W. Norton, 2010), 10.

Martin E.P. Seligman . . . PERMA John Tierney, "A New Gauge to See What's Beyond Happiness," *New York Times* (May 17, 2011): D2.

research at Stanford University on the effects of suppressing emotion Daniel Goleman, *Social Intelligence*, 21.

"The tension was not just palpable . . ." Daniel Goleman, *Social Intelligence*, 21.

Facial expressions are a key part of our emotion-detection system Paul Ekman, "Facial Expression and Emotion," *American Psychologist* 48, no. 4 (April 1993): 384-92; Daniel Goleman, *Social Intelligence*, 43.

the ability to read those signals http://www.paulekman.com.

Deception is part of being human Michael Gazzaniga, *Human: The Science Behind What Makes Us Unique* (New York: Ecco/HarperCollins, 2008), 102.

Edgar Allan Poe, in his short story Edgar Allan Poe, "The Purloined Letter" (1845), accessed at http://xroads.virginia.edu/~hyper/poe/purloine.html.

Researchers in Richard Davidson's lab Antoine Lutz, Lawrence L. Greischar, Nancy B. Rawlings, Matthieu Ricard, and Richard J. Davidson, "Long-term Meditators Self-induce High-amplitude Gamma Synchrony During Mental Practice," *Proceedings of the National Academy of Sciences* 101, no. 46 (November 16, 2004): 16369-373.

"We do better if we are surrounded . . . enlightened self-interest" Frans de Waal, "The Evolution of Empathy," *Greater Good* 2, issue 2 (Fall/Winter 2005-06): 4.

There's a study of helping behavior John M. Darley and C. Daniel Batson, "'From Jerusalem to Jericho': A Study of Situational and Dispositional Variables in Helping Behavior," *Journal of Personality and Social Psychology* 27, no.1 (July 1973): 100-103.

One doctor, a gynecologist, recalled Katie Hafner, "Dr. Anyone, Summoned to Duty at 30,000 Feet," *New York Times* (May 24, 2011): D1.

by just three degrees of separation Nicholas A. Christakis, MD, PhD, and James H. Fowler, PhD, *Connected: The Surprising Power of Our Social Networks and How They Shape Our Lives* (New York: Little, Brown, 2009), 28-9.

"Social networks have value . . ." Christakis and Fowler, 31.

"share and increase the very good they have received" Robert Emmons, "Pay It Forward," in *The Compassionate Instinct*, ed. Keltner and others, 77.

"I've concluded that gratitude . . ." Robert Emmons, 80.

Social networks "tend to magnify . . ." Christakis and Fowler, 31.

"influence the spread of joy . . ." Christakis and Fowler, 31.

On the negative side, they can spread Christakis and Fowler, 31.

"In our youth, they help us . . ." Aristotle, *Aristotle: Selections from Seven of the Most Important Books*, 7th ed., trans. Philip Wheelwright (New York: The Odyssey Press, 1951), 236.

A columnist for *Town & Country* **lamented** Joan Caraganis Jakobson, "Where Have All the Presents Gone?" *Town & Country* (December 2008): 186.

we have more difficulty distinguishing individuals James W. Tanaka, Markus Kiefer, and Cindy Bukach, "A Holistic Account of Own-Race Effect in Face Recognition: Evidence from a Cross-Cultural Study," *Cognition*, no. 93 (2004): B1-B9.

"I found that everybody wants the same thing—validation" Oprah Winfrey, "The Oprah Winfrey Show," aired May 25, 2011.

In a study at the University of Michigan Diane Swanbrow, "Empathy: College Students Don't Have as Much as They Used To," accessed at http://michigan today.umich.edu/2010/06/story.php?id=7777.

"By the imagination we place ourselves ..." Adam Smith, *The Theory of Moral Sentiments* (Cambridge UK: Cambridge University Press, 2002), 12.

CHAPTER 4—WHY MANNERS MATTER

"The work of etiquette is to socialize ... springs" Hazel Barnes, "Take Clothes, For Example," in *Etiquette: Reflections on Contemporary Comportment*, ed. Ron Scapp and Brian Seitz, (Albany: State University of New York Press, 2007), 239.

"Manners are what vex or soothe ..." Edmund Burke, "Two Letters Addressed to a Member of the Present Parliament on the Proposals for Peace with the Regicide Directory of France, Letter I: On the Overtures of Peace," in *Burke: Select Works*, ed. E. J. Payne, MA (Oxford UK: Clarendon Press, 1878), 72.

"is the oldest social virtue ..." Judith Martin, "The World's Oldest Virtue," *First Things* (May 1993): 22-5. Accessed at http://www.firstthings.com/article/2008/08/003-the-worlds-oldest-virtue-38.

"socially challenged" Caroline Tiger, *How to Behave: A Guide to Modern Manners for the Socially Challenged* (Philadelphia: Quirk Books, 2003).

Even the august Massachusetts Institute of Technology Charm School website, MIT Student Activities Office, accessed at http://studentlife.mit.edu/sao/charm.

"Manners are a sensitive awareness ..." The Emily Post Institute, http://www.emilypost.com/everyday-manners/guidelines-for-living/454-emily-post-quotations.

called manners "factitious" Ralph Waldo Emerson, *The Conduct of Life* (Boston: Houghton Mifflin, 1903; New York: AMS, 1979), 174. Citations are to AMS edition.

"persons of character" Ralph Waldo Emerson, 188.

"Be kind to animals ... feelings too" Munro Leaf, *Manners Can Be Fun*. (New York: Universe, 1936), 38-9.

"When I play with other girls . . ." Munro Leaf, 29.

"Having good manners . . ." Munro Leaf, 7.

"I want to change the world . . ." Mitzi Taylor, Not So Common Courtesy website, http://www.notsocommoncourtesy.com.

"There are certain manners . . ." Ralph Waldo Emerson, 170.

Lucinda Holdforth cites a chilling case Lucinda Holdforth, *Why Manners Matter: The Case for Civilized Behavior in a Barbarous World* (New York: Amy Einhorn Books, 2007), 59.

"Manners are very communicable . . ." Ralph Waldo Emerson, 170.

"Manners are used to establish . . ." Judith Martin, "The World's Oldest Virtue."

"What are they but thoughts entering . . ." Ralph Waldo Emerson, 171.

"righteously hounding" smokers Judith Martin, *Miss Manners' Guide to Excruciatingly Correct Behavior* (New York: W. W. Norton, 2005), 745.

Miss Manners is herself "unfailingly polite" Judith Martin, *Miss Manners' Guide*, 22.

"meager arsenal," consisting of "the withering look . . ." Judith Martin, *Miss Manners' Guide*, 23.

"the ability to dismiss . . ." Judith Martin, *Miss Manners' Guide*, 23.

"If you are rude to your ex-husband's . . ." Judith Martin, *Miss Manners' Guide*, 25.

"like those with whom we do not feel frightened . . ." Aristotle, *Rhetoric 2*, chapter 4, in *The Complete Works of Aristotle: The Revised Oxford Translation*, ed. Jonathan Barnes, Bollingen Series, vol. 2 (London: Oxford University Press, 1984), 2201.

"charming" manners "which immediately gave one a feeling . . ." Roy R. Grinker, MD, "Reminiscences of a Personal Contact with Freud," *American Journal of Orthopsychiatry* 10, issue 4 (October 1940): 850.

"It is our nature to enjoy giving . . ." Marshall Rosenberg, *Nonviolent Communication: A Language of Life*, 2nd ed. (Encinitas CA: PuddleDancer Press, 2003), 1.

"Adab is courtesy . . ." Kabir Helminski, "Adab: The Courtesy of the Path," adapted from traditional sources. Accessed at http://www.sufism.org/books/sacred/adab.html.

"the concentrated essence . . ." Andrew Harvey, interviewed by Frederic A. Brussat, "Adab: All Good Traits Combined," *Spirituality & Practice* online, http://www.spiritualityandpractice.com/practices/features.php?id=17521.

"that is the perfection of adab ... any reward from it" Andrew Harvey, *Spirituality & Practice*.

"a nobility of character ..." Andrew Harvey, *Spirituality & Practice*.

adab—"to prepare a banquet ..." "Adab in the Mevlevi Tradition," http://www.dar-al-masnavi.org/adab-mevlevi.html.

"impression management" Erving Goffman, *The Presentation of Self in Everyday Life* (New York: Anchor Books, 1959), 208.

"Regardless of the particular objective ..." Erving Goffman, 3.

CHAPTER 5—LOVE, LOVE ME DO

to love and to work Sigmund Freud, *Civilization and Its Discontents*, James Strachey, trans. (New York: Routledge, 2005), 88.

"Romantic love is a human drive ..." Helen Fisher, *Why Him? Why Her?: Finding Real Love by Understanding Your Personality Type* (New York: Henry Holt, 2009), 221.

relationships that begin with instant attraction Earl Naumann, *Love at First Sight: The Stories and Science Behind Instant Attraction* (Naperville IL: Sourcebooks, 2001), ix.

her "best guy friend," as she describes him Rose Peterson, interviewed by Tony Gervino, *New York Times Magazine* (May 29, 2011): 20.

"Rose was a great date ..." Gabriel Luciano-Carson, interviewed by Tony Gervino, *New York Times Magazine*, 20.

Fisher came up with a personality typology Helen Fisher, *Why Him? Why Her?*, 9-12.

identified the activities of neurotransmitters Helen Fisher, *Why We Love: The Nature and Chemistry of Romantic Love* (New York: Henry Holt, 2004), 51-76.

the adventurous, "drink life to the fullest" Explorer Helen Fisher, *Why Him? Why Her?*, 9-17.

one-tenth of a second to form a first impression Janine Willis and Alexander Todorov, "First Impressions: Making Up Your Mind After a 100-Ms Exposure to a Face," *Psychological Science* 17, no. 7 (2006): 592-98.

as little as three minutes of talking . . . Helen Fisher, "The Realities of Love at First Sight," *O, the Oprah Magazine* (November 2009), accessed at http://www.oprah.com/relationships/Love-at-First-Sight-Helen-Fisher-Love-Column.

"Rule-breakers are exciting . . . adrenaline running" Philip Hodson, quoted in "Focus: Why We Love a Bad Boy," *The Independent,* August 28, 2005. Accessed at http://www.independent.co.uk/news/uk/this-britain/focus-why-we-love-a-bad-boy-504565.html.

studied women's preference for "cads" versus "dads" Sigal Tifferet and Daniel J. Kruger, "The Terminal Investment Hypothesis and Age-related Differences in Female Preference for Dads vs. Cads," *Letters on Evolutionary Behavioral Science* 1, no. 2 (2010): 27-30.

The median age at first marriage D'Vera Cohn, "The State of Love and Marriage," Pew Research Center Publications, October 15, 2009. http://pewresearch.org/pubs/1380/marriage-and-divorce-by-state.

study of men and women in thirty-seven different cultures David M. Buss, "Strategies of Human Mating," *Psychological Topics* 15, no. 2 (2006): 244.

Fisher defines agreeableness Helen Fisher, *Why Him? Why Her?,* 115.

estrogen activity is behind the "web thinking" Helen Fisher, *Why Him? Why Her?,* 105.

Negotiator's best shot at compatibility Helen Fisher, *Why Him? Why Her?,* 185.

tendency to be nosy and overly involved Helen Fisher, *Why Him? Why Her?,* 121-22.

"The chemistry of romantic love . . ." Helen Fisher, *Why We Love,* 86.

to facilitate interpersonal behavior Michael Kosfeld, Markus Heinrichs, Paul J. Zak, Urs Fischbacher, and Ernst Fehr, "Oxytocin Increases Trust in Humans," *Nature* 435, no. 2 (June 2005): 673-76.

promoting generosity during research Paul J. Zak, Angela A. Stanton, and Sheila Ahmadi, "Oxytocin Increases Generosity in Humans," *PLoS ONE* 2, no. 11 (November 2007): e1128. Accessed at http://www.plosone.org/article/info:doi%2F10.1371%2Fjournal.pone.0001128.

modulating the anxiety associated with romantic love Donatella Marazziti, Bernardo Dell'Osso, Stefano Baroni, Francesco Mungai, Mario Catena, Paola Rucci, Francesco Albanese, et al, "A Relationship Between Oxytocin and

Anxiety of Romantic Attachment," Clinical Practice and Epidemiology in Mental Health 2, no.1 (2002): 28. Accessed at http://www.cpemental health.com/content/2/1/28.

the secret to long-time commitment Arthur Aron and Elaine N. Aron, *Love and the Expansion of Self: Understanding Attraction and Satisfaction* (New York: Hemisphere/Harper & Row, 1986).

"novel and arousing activities" Arthur Aron, Christina C. Norman, Elaine N. Aron, Colin McKenna, and Richard Heyman, "Couples' Shared Participation in Novel and Arousing Activities and Experienced Relationship Quality," *Journal of Personality and Social Psychology* 78, no. 2 (2000): 273.

physical activity involving gym mats and Velcro straps Arthur Aron, Christina C. Norman, and others, 279.

genetic makers of marital instability Tara Parker-Pope, "The Science of a Happy Marriage," *New York Times* (May 11, 2010): 1D.

"Q: My husband works for a hedge fund . . ." E. Jean Carroll, "Ask E. Jean," Elle.com, http://www.elle.com/Life-Love/Ask-E.-Jean/Ask-EJean-Husbandly-Duties.

"Threatening circumstances" mobilize us faster Harry T. Reis and Shelly L. Gable, "Toward a Positive Psychology of Relationships," in *Flourishing: Positive Psychology and the Life Well-Lived*, ed. Corey L. M. Keyes and Jonathan Haidt (Washington, DC: American Psychological Association, 2003), 136.

both men and women put "kindness and understanding" at the top David M. Buss, "Human Mate Selection," *American Scientist* 73 (January-February 1985): 48.

wikiHow organizes its advice into six basic "Steps" "How to Love," http://www.wikihow.com/Love.

divorce rate in America still hovers between 45 and 50 percent "Quick Facts: America and Divorce," http://www.presstv.ir/usdetail/170458.html.

A woman who had been married for a year Philip Galanes, "Can't Brush It Away," *New York Times* (December 27, 2009): ST6.

Arthur Aron offers another analogy Kasia Galazka, "The Biology of a Breakup," *Psychology Today* (April 2011): 19.

our-marriage-is-over-but-we're-still-living-together Carol Mithers, "Divorce, Interrupted," *O, the Oprah Magazine* (May 2009): 133-34.

One couple even threw a divorce party Geraldine Fabrikant, "Divorce, in Style," *New York Times* (May 15, 2011): ST9.

"As we change the parameters of our relationship . . ." Geraldine Fabrikant, ST9.

"But so also is the capacity for forgiveness" Michael McCullough, "Forgiveness," in *The Compassionate Instinct,* ed. Dacher Keltner, Jason Marsh, and Jeremy Adam Smith (New York: W. W. Norton, 2010), 53.

"I know you're perfectly capable of living . . ." Louise Rafkin, "Kestrin Pantera and Jonathan Grubb," *New York Times.* (April 11, 2010): ST14.

CHAPTER 6—WHEN KINDNESS GOES TO WORK

"If you bring joy and enthusiasm . . ." William Haefeli, cartoon, *New Yorker* (May 9, 2011): 49.

wrote a little book in 2006 Linda Kaplan Thaler and Robin Koval, *The Power of Nice: How to Conquer the Business World with Kindness* (New York: Currency/Doubleday, 2006).

Harvard Business Review published an article Tiziana Casciaro and Miguel Sousa Lobo, "Competent Jerks, Lovable Fools, and the Formation of Social Networks," *Harvard Business Review.* (June 2005): 1-9.

"her personal touch, her ability to reach out . . ." Kevin Conley, "What She Saw at the Revolution," *Vogue* (May 2010): 229.

"She really sets an example . . ." Kevin Conley, 229.

"My father always taught me . . ." Alberto Perlman, as told to Patricia R. Olsen, "Born for Business," *New York Times* (May 23, 2010): BU10.

Clothing manufacturer Eileen Fisher "Eileen Fisher—The Wholeness Philosophy," Leading with Kindness website (July 7, 2008). Accessed at http://www.wliw.org/leadingwithkindness/profile/eileen-fisher/35/.

The gesture not only "feels right" Susan Schor, quoted in "Eileen Fisher—The Wholeness Philosophy."

PrintingForLess.com, an online printing services company Shayla McKnight, as told to Patricia R. Olsen, "Workplace Gossip? Keep It To Yourself," *New York Times* (November 11, 2009): BU9.

"Nice must be automatic" Linda Kaplan Thaler and Robin Koval, 10.

Stanislavski's system for actors Sondra Thiederman, PhD, "The 'Magic If': Achieving Empathy in Your Diverse Workplace," adapted from *Making Diversity Work: Seven Steps for Defeating Bias in the Workplace* (Chicago: Dearborn Press, 2003), accessed at www.workforcediversitynetwork.com/res _expertforum_theiderman.aspx.

qualities like humility, gratitude, humor, and compassion William Baker and Michael O'Malley, "Discovering Leading with Kindness," Leading with Kindness website. http://www.wliw.org/leadingwithkindness/about/ essays/discovering-leading-with-kindness/.

Zappos, the online shoe store, is one Tony Hsieh, *Delivering Happiness* (New York: Business Plus, 2010); Alexandra Jacobs, "Happy Feet," *New Yorker* (September 14, 2009): 66-71.

Random Acts of Kindness Parade "Zappos Chronicles: Random Acts of Kindness Parade," video, http://blogs.zappos.com/blogs/zappos-tv/2008/08/ 04/zappos-chronicles-random-acts-of-kindness-parade.

CHAPTER 7—DIGITAL LIFE

Youngsters age eighteen and under Tamar Lewin, "If Your Kids Are Awake, They're Probably Online," *New York Times* (January 20, 2010): A1.

Sherry Turkle . . . spent five years interviewing children Julie Scelfo, "R U Here, Mom?," *New York Times* (June 10, 2010): D1.

Daniel Goleman . . . started off a column Daniel Goleman, "E-Mail Is Easy to Write (and to Misread)," *New York Times* (October 7, 2007): B17.

"online disinhibition effect" John Suler, PhD, "The Online Disinhibition Effect," *CyberPsychology & Behavior* 7, no. 3 (2004): 321.

"show unusual acts of kindness and generosity . . ." John Suler, 321.

YouTube video of the woman falling headfirst into a fountain "Texting While Walking, Woman Falls into Fountain." CBS News online, http://www .cbsnews.com/stories/2011/01/20/earlyshow/main7265096.shtml; "Texting Fail: Woman Falls in Fountain," CBS News video, uploaded to YouTube on January 20, 2011, http://www.youtube.com/watch?v=ZXYY_ep5Nh0.

Oprah launched a "No Phone Zone Pledge" Oprah Winfrey, "Text at Your Own Risk," Oprah.com, http://www.oprah.com/packages/no-phone-zone.html.

psychiatrist, describing various ways her patients handle calls Barbara Schildkrout, "In Therapy, Cellphones Ring True," *New York Times* (March 23, 2010): D5.

established "cell phone-free Sundays" Meredith Melnick, *Time* Healthland, November 23, 2010, http://healthland.time.com/2010/11/23/turning-your-phone-off-as-a-technological-gesture-of-affection/.

instituted a national Day of Unplugging Austin Considine, "And on the Sabbath, the iPhones Shall Rest," *New York Times* (March 18, 2010): E6.

what Reboot dubbed the Ten Principles "The Ten Principles," Sabbath Manifesto website, http://www.sabbathmanifesto.org.

"Amazingly calming" Anna, Sabbath Manifesto website, http://www.sabbath manifesto.org/community.

"Wholesome, insightful, and refreshing" Will Sloan, Sabbath Manifesto website.

"I saw some friends ..." Tanya Schevitz, "Josh Radnor Connects to Life Old School Style," *Huffington Post* (May 4, 2010). http://www.huffingtonpost.com/tanya-schevitz/josh-radnor-connects-to_l_b_562890.html.

limited-edition "cell phone sleeping bag" "Unplug with Your Sabbath Manifesto Cell Phone Sleeping Bag," Sabbath Manifesto website, http://www.sabbathmanifesto.org/unplug/.

"the Phonekerchief" The Neat Geek, http://www.neatgeek.net/disconnect-with-the-phonekerchief.html.

"We may be sitting at the same table ..." Ingrid Zwiefel, www.myphoneisoff foryou.com. [dead link]

Emily Gould was twenty-four when she launched her blog Emily Gould, "Exposed," *New York Times Magazine* (May 25, 2008): 32.

praised its "infinite potential for connection" Peggy Orenstein, "I Tweet, Therefore I Am," *New York Times Magazine* (August 1, 2010): 12.

"When every thought is externalized ..." Peggy Orenstein, 12.

"virtuosos of self-presentation" Sherry Turkle, "Can You Hear Me Now?" Forbes .com (May 7, 2007), http://www.forbes.com/forbes/2007/0507/176.html.

"We'd rather text than talk" Sherry Turkle, *Alone Together: Why We Expect More from Technology and Less from Each Other* (New York: Basic Books, 2011): 1.

gossip **"is the core of human social relationships"** Robin I.M. Dunbar, "Gossip in Evolutionary Perspective," *Review of General Psychology* 8, no.2 (June 2004): 100.

"unprecedented ability to establish . . . who is closer" Michael Rogers, "How Social Can We Get?" msnbc.com (September 10, 2007), http://www.msnbc .msn.com/id/7213382.

Privacy settings only go so far Steve Lohr, "How Privacy Can Vanish Online, a Bit at a Time," *New York Times* (March 17, 2010): A3.

time we spent on social networking sites increased "Are Social Networking Sites Good for Our Society?" ProCon.org, http://socialnetworking.pro con.org.

"Having two identities for yourself . . ." Miguel Helft, "Facebook, Foe of Anonymity, Is Forced to Explain a Secret," *New York Times* (May 14, 2011): B1.

the maximum number of friends Robin Dunbar, *How Many Friends Does One Person Need?: Dunbar's Number and Other Evolutionary Quirks* (Cambridge MA: Harvard University Press, 2010), 24.

When we're online . . . bit of brain machinery Daniel Goleman, "Flame First, Think Later: New Clues to E-Mail Misbehavior," *New York Times* (February 20, 2007). Accessed at http://www.nytimes.com/2007/02/20/health/ psychology/20essa.html.

none of society's usual "rules" curbing us online John Suler, 323.

The actor John Cusack, an enthusiastic tweeter John Metcalfe, "On the Twitter Patrol," *New York Times* (April 29, 2010): E8.

"In the search for sharing . . ." Pope Benedict XVI, "Truth, Proclamation, and Authenticity of Life in the Digital Age," message for World Commu-nications Day, June 5, 2011. *Catholic New York* 30, no. 10 (January 27, 2011): 13.

Online services are popping up Jenna Wortham, "Focusing on the Social, Minus the Media," *New York Times* (June 5, 2011): BU4.

"There is a kind of social media . . ." "MOST UNWANTED—Global," *Monocle* 3, issue 29 (January/February 2010): 36.

CHAPTER 8—TOO NICE FOR YOUR OWN GOOD

"scarily prevalent issue" Lena Corner, "Time to Get Tough: How Being Nasty Can Improve Your Life," *The Independent* (March 9, 2008). Accessed at http://www.independent.co.uk/arts-entertainment/books/features/time-to-get-tough-how-being-nasty-can-improve-your-life-792446.html.

people think they are about to lose their options Jiwoong Shin and Dan Ariely, "Keeping Doors Open: The Effect of Unavailability on Incentives to Keep Options Viable," *Management Science* 50, no. 5 (May 2004): 575-86.

There's a Korean horror movie, *301/302* Tina Chanter, "Eating Dogs and Women: Abject Rules of Etiquette in *301/302*," in *Etiquette: Reflections on Contemporary Comportment*, ed. Ron Scapp and Brian Seitz (Albany: State University of New York Press, 2007), 95-104.

most people won't need to go as far Martin Kihn, *A$$hole: How I Got Rich & Happy by Not Giving a Damn About Anyone and How You Can Too* (New York: Broadway Books, 2008).

"I was the nicest guy in the world" Martin Kihn, 3.

"I prefer an interesting vice . . ." Molière (Jean-Baptiste Poquelin), ThinkExist .com, http://www.thinkexist.com/quotation/i_prefer_an_interesting _vice_to_a_virtue_that/170343.html.

"Without negativity . . . drive others away" Barbara Fredrickson, PhD, *Positivity: Groundbreaking Research Reveals How to Embrace the Hidden Strength of Positive Emotions, Overcome Negativity, and Thrive* (New York: Crown, 2009), 136.

House, the brilliant but irascible doctor Mélanie Frappier, "Nice Is Overrated," *TPM: The Philosopher's Magazine*, issue 43 (November 2009). Edited and abridged from *House and Philosophy: Everybody Lies*, ed. Henry Jacoby, Blackwell Philosophy and Popular Culture Series (Hoboken NJ: Wiley, 2008). Accessed at www.philosophypress.co.uk/?p=861.

we come off as insincere Margaret Visser, *The Gift of Thanks: The Roots, Persistence, and Paradoxical Meanings of a Social Ritual* (New York: HarperCollins, 2008), 7.

"their virtuous deeds mask insecurity" Christopher Peterson and Martin E. P. Seligman, *Character Strengths and Virtues: A Handbook and Classification*

(Washington DC: American Psychological Association and New York: Oxford University Press, 2004), 21.

"The real sin . . . the part of the sinner" Peterson and Seligman, 21.

The genuine, or so-called Duchenne smile Paul Ekman, Richard J. Davidson, and Wallace V. Friesen, "The Duchenne Smile: Emotional Expression and Brain Physiology II," *Journal of Personality and Social Psychology* 58, no. 2 (February 1990): 342.

CONCLUSION—ARE WE NICE YET?

Kind comes from the Middle English word *kynde* *The American Heritage Dictionary of the English Language*, ed. William Morris (New York: American Heritage Publishing Company and Boston: Houghton Mifflin, 1969), 721, 1516.

"I think it's important to work . . ." Rebecca Murray, About.com, Natalie Portman interview, *Black Swan* press conference (November 2010). http://movies .about.com/od/blackswan/a/Natalie-Portman-Black-Swan.htm.

even diehard techies are beginning to yearn Jenna Wortham, "Focusing on the Social, Minus the Media," *New York Times*. (June 5, 2011): BU4.

ACKNOWLEDGMENTS

Deepest thanks to Emily Rapoport, my editor at Berkley, who had the idea for a book on *nice* in the first place—and was unfailingly patient and cheerful during months of waiting for the manuscript. Thanks, too, to my friend Joel Fotinos, a vice president at Penguin and publisher of Tarcher/Penguin, for recommending me to Emily. And special thanks to my agent, Stephanie Tade, a steadying force throughout the process, especially during the last mad weeks of racing to the finish line.

Thanks to my neighbor Marion Moskowitz Moss for the conversation that opens the book, and to Mark Matousek, who said two magic words—*mirror neurons*—that unlocked the social side of *nice*.

Very special thanks to the Nice Report Survey participants and all the people who shared tales of their encounters with the *nice* and *not-so-nice*. The book would literally be nothing without the contributions of Alice Allen, Heide Banks, Anna Bernhard, Barbara Biziou, Rande Brown, Chester Burger, George Castanis, Betsy Castle, Lyman Castle, Mia Castle, Cheryl Chalmers, Kara Fanelli, John Foreman, Adam Friedman, Heidi G., Patty Gift, Barbara Grande, Melora Griffis, Dana Grunklee, Don Harrell, Rachel Hiles, John House, Alex Ionescu, Alex Kaloyanides, Mary Landers, Laurie Laughren, Cyndi Lee, Alex Marshall, Meg Morse, Sam Mowe, Hugh Tenkan O'Hare, Bunny Oliver, Sara Overton, Gina Raimondi, Emily Rapoport, Scott Russell, Phil Ryan, Sharon Salzberg, Bob Saxton, Karl Schuman, Nicole Shaver, Donysha Smith, Leonard Sorcher, Tyler Soroka, Clark Strand, Stephanie Tade, Sandra Weinberg, Eleanor Wiley, and two others who wish to remain anonymous.

Thanks always to the nicest friends one could hope for. Nearly a decade ago, Andrew Harvey and I traded ideas for a book on spiritual etiquette; some of them found their way into the chapter on manners. Sharon Salzberg offered insight on *nice* from years of experience as a meditation teacher. Mary Landers read drafts and provided valuable feedback along with countless home-cooked dinners, walks to the dog park, and much-needed laughter. Patty Gift, incisive editor and heart sister as generous as her name, was ever ready with a fresh perspective, expert advice, and cinematic diversion. John House very generously set up the Nice Report website, patiently demystifying computer technology.

I'm indebted to Daniel Goleman, Marco Iacoboni, Michael

Gazzaniga, Jonathan Haidt, and others for their clear exposition of current research in psychology and neuroscience.

Thanks to Health S.O.S. for unknotting my aching body after endless hours at the computer. Special appreciation to physical therapists Hana Liebowitz and Kara Fanelli, trainers Adam Friedman and Matt Blye, and scheduling/insurance maven Nicole Shaver.

Finally, thanks to my family: Susie and Ned Montgomery; the late Bunny Oliver; Betsy Castle; Jerry, Trinity, and Bella Haddam; Mia Castle; Dakota and Duncan Mackey; Molly, Duane, and Matthew Napolitana; Meg, John, and Toby Morse; Lyman, Rachel, Andrew, and Charlie Castle; Tim and Claire Barnett. They epitomize *nice* in all the ways the book describes.

CREDITS

..............................— • —..............................

Grateful acknowledgment is made to the following for permission to reprint previously published material:

The New York Times: Excerpt from "E-Mail is Easy to Write (And to Misread)" from *The New York Times*, October 7, 2007, copyright © 2007 by *The New York Times*. All rights reserved. Reprinted by permission of *The New York Times* and protected by the copyright laws of the United States. The printing, copying, redistribution, or retransmission of this content without express written permission is prohibited.

Rizzoli International Publications, Inc.: Excerpts from *Manners Can Be Fun* by Munro Leaf, copyright © 1936 by Munro Leaf. Reprinted by permission of Rizzoli International Publications, Inc.

The Zen Studies Society: Excerpt from *Sutra Book*, copyright © 1982 by The Zen Studies Society. Reprinted by permission of The Zen Studies Society and Shinge Roshi, Roko Sherry Chayat.

Reboot, Inc.: "The Ten Principles," excerpted from Sabbath Manifesto, http://